It falls to someone to document the truth.

THE WAR ON DRUGS EXPLAINED

Matthew Fraser

CONTENTS

PREFACE

I have had a fascination with all things 'drugs' for my entire adult life. My first significant recollection of this consuming interest was an event in the mid 1980s when the news arrived that two Australians had been executed by hanging due to involvement with an illicit drug: namely heroin.

I remember at the time that those around me were generally unsympathetic to the fate of the two saying they knew of the possible consequences before choosing to be involved in such activities. In other words, they should have been deterred by the knowledge that it might cost them their lives and, essentially, that their killing was justifiable in some way.

At the time, I could not understand why two people would be subject to execution due to being involved with a drug of choice. What could the justification be for killing two people who were apparently involved in the supply of a substance that people took voluntarily for its effects as do so many who use alcohol, tobacco, and caffeine?

It is conveyed to us that the supply and use of heroin must be resolutely prevented and discouraged to the extent of providing apparent justification for capital punishment in some countries. The rationale given for this strategy, then and to this day, is that heroin is capable of causing sudden death due to the simple act of taking 'too much' (in other words, an overdose). We are told people's breathing is impaired to a degree that results in injury or death. However, I now know this is nonsense and a lie so malevolent and dangerous so as to actually make it more likely that deaths occur due to the combining of central nervous system depressant drugs.

What made the occurrence so perplexing for me, in part, was the fact that I was surrounded by drug use: the enthusiastic and unquestioned use of alcohol, tobacco and caffeine. Australian society has always been one in which the use of these three drugs is absolutely ingrained. Alcohol and caffeine are essentially worshipped and accepted as an integral part of life for many. That every person has immediate and unimpeded access to these drugs is a situation unable to be questioned without eliciting indignation and derision.

Australian culture is one in which the use of alcohol is normalised to the degree that its consumption is almost expected. As a generalisation, people who do not consume alcohol are held in suspicion verging on contempt by those who do. It is generally accepted as a rite of passage for the young to drink to excess, vomit and suffer a hangover.

Again, and accordingly fuelling my interest and confusion, why would people from a culture in which drug use is so normalised and widespread accept and even condone the killing of two people due to their involvement in the supply of a recreational drug? Even at that time, the hypocrisy and double standards were apparent to me even though my understanding of the situation was rudimentary.

As the decades went by and my understanding of the subject increased in line with my fascination, nothing changed. People were still being imprisoned and executed ostensibly for involvement in the supply or possession of a drug of choice.

As time has progressed, however, my understanding has increased to a point where I have come to a realisation of the actual nature of the so-called 'War on Drugs'. With this understanding has come an increased horror and bewilderment regarding the capacity of human beings to exploit and be cruel to each other in the pursuit of financial gain and political advantage.

Throughout history, the capability and willingness of humans to engage in cruelty to each other and to other species is amply demonstrated. One would have thought, obviously with a great deal of naivety, that humanity would have learnt from this and endeavoured to make the world a better and less cruel place.

Not so. The 'War on Drugs' grinds on and gathers momentum whilst being justified as a mechanism to protect health and welfare. But just as disturbingly, there is complete and intentional suppression and denial of the actual nature of the phenomenon. It is, in fact, possibly the greatest act of political fraud that has ever been played on humanity.

Fifty years on from the intensification of the policy by the United States under the stewardship of President Richard Nixon, the truth about it remains nonexistent in the public domain. Those with an interest in the policy continuing ensure that every falsehood and method of obfuscation is employed to conceal its true nature and prevent genuine discussion about it occurring.

I have grown increasingly frustrated over the years regarding the lack of honesty on the subject and it is clear that the truth needs to be publicly communicated for there to be any chance of real discussion and change. I have never encountered a conversation or any literature in the public arena that genuinely and openly examines the reality of the phenomenon. Every discussion or opinion is tainted either by naivety or a knowing coyness prompted by self-interest.

My frustration drove me to create the website drugtruthinternational.org as a means of publicly documenting the truth about various subjects within the realms of psychoactive-substance use and human rights. This book is my continued effort to have the truth documented and accessible.

A worldwide human-rights abuse has been in progress for many decades whilst being portrayed as a legitimate strategy. Obviously, this is not an acceptable situation. The true motives and consequences of the policy must be openly and widely communicated because what is happening is beyond abhorrent.

This book is the culmination of a life's interest and fascination and a way of documenting the truth because it, the 'War on Drugs', needs to be recognised for what it actually is.

INTRODUCTION

The purpose of this book is to put on record the true nature of the policy regime known as the 'War on Drugs'. The phenomenon is portrayed by those who benefit from it as a strategy to protect health and welfare in relation to the use of psychoactive substances or what are universally referred to as 'drugs'. Nothing could be further from the truth.

It would perhaps be justifiable to describe the 'War on Drugs' as the organised human-rights abuse that has defined the last fifty years. In its current form, the policy has been ravaging the world since the early 1970s. From people being executed, to hundreds of thousands incarcerated, it is an atrocity that occurs on a worldwide basis due to compliance with its application being achieved essentially without exception.

This book is prompted by the fact that discussion on the true nature of the policy is completely taboo. The dominant narrative comprises an assertion that it is a failure in relation to its stated motives and should be altered so as to be less oppressive on those affected by it.

This narrative is, like the 'War on Drugs' itself, a complete and utter deception and promoted by those who benefit financially from the policy and, accordingly, wish for it to continue.

The so-called 'War on Drugs' is not a failure and it is not a mistake. It is absolutely intentional and is categorically successful in relation to its actual motives.

An understanding of the malevolent nature of the phenomenon and its devastating effect on humanity cannot be achieved if it is assumed to be a strategy that holds true to its apparent objectives. Those who do not have an understanding of the true nature of the policy deserve to have the truth documented so, at the very least, they have the opportunity to consider it based upon a comprehension of its actual motives and consequences.

It is not acceptable under any circumstances for the truth about the 'War on Drugs' to not be effectively communicated. The policy causes suffering on a scale that is almost unimaginable by enabling oppression and economic utilisation of those who are simply members of a minority and, therefore, vulnerable to being treated inequitably.

This book endeavours to provide an account of the true nature of the so-called 'War on Drugs' in a succinct and direct manner. The numerous myths, deceptions and falsehoods are explained so that the reader can gain a realistic perspective on the policy and, thereby, come to understand its actual intentions and consequences. Importantly, the various people, professions and organisations who benefit from the regime are identified and the nature of their self-interest in the policy is discussed.

My hope is that this book prompts people to critically examine any assumptions they may have about the intentions of the policy and, thereby, allows for understanding that will form the basis for change. An end to the atrocity that is the 'War on Drugs' is necessary, easily achieved and would deliver a considerably more equitable and peaceful world.

TERMINOLOGY

I have used a variety of terms in reference to non-food substances taken voluntarily for their effects on the central nervous system in a non-medical context. Such terms are 'drug', 'recreational drug', 'substance' and 'psychoactive substance'. I would like to emphasise that alcohol, tobacco and caffeine are taken voluntarily for their effects on the central nervous system in a non-medical context and are therefore, by their very nature, drugs and psychoactive substances.

The term 'opioid' is used in reference to morphine and morphine-like substances of natural, semi-synthetic or synthetic origin that activate opioid receptors in the central nervous system.

The term 'criminalised' is used in reference to a situation in which people are made liable to penalty from the criminal justice system due to a particular behaviour they engage in.

The term 'public money' is used in reference to money collected and held by governments.

I would like to put on record that I do not use drugs that are defined as illicit. I also do not use alcohol or tobacco and caffeine consumption is a rarity. I have not written this book from the perspective of personal substance use.

THE BASICS

People who use alcohol, tobacco, and caffeine can use their substance without fear of being punished by society. They can use their drug freely and without penalty from the criminal justice system. They can possess and use their drug of choice and not be subject to any of the following: arrest, being brought before a court, being fined, having a criminal record imposed upon them or imprisonment. They will not suffer discrimination or be disadvantaged in any way due to their use of a recreational drug.

THE FUNDAMENTAL QUESTION

Why are people who supply and use drugs other than alcohol, tobacco and caffeine criminalised in respect of their drug-related activities when the suppliers and users of alcohol, tobacco, and caffeine are not?

The answer given by governments and their agents is that suppliers and users of drugs other than alcohol, tobacco and caffeine are criminalised in order to provide for punishment and deterrence regarding supply and use of the substances on the basis of preventing and minimising harm to health and welfare.

The substances are essentially portrayed as a threat to mankind requiring control and eradication: hence the 'War on Drugs'. The flagship substance in the portrayal of drugs other than alcohol, tobacco and caffeine as being uniquely dangerous is heroin. The decades-old assertion is that the substance is responsible for the sudden deaths of people who take 'too much'.

However, the assertion that the so-called 'War on Drugs' is a response to harm caused to health and welfare by the use of psychoactive substances is a complete deception. The following two pieces of information are fundamental to understanding why the stated rationale for the policy regime is untrue.

Firstly, the two most dangerous drugs in existence are undeniably alcohol and tobacco. The use of these two substances leads to the vast majority of drug-related mortality and a huge burden of disease.

Alcohol is so toxic it kills bacteria on contact: hence its use as a disinfectant. It is associated with organ disease including brain and liver damage and undesirable behaviour such as violence, sexual assault and dangerous driving due to its disinhibitory effects. Alcohol consumption during pregnancy can result in Fetal Alcohol Spectrum Disorder with the child suffering from a syndrome comprising a variety of neurodevelopmental and physical deficits.

When smoked, tobacco introduces scores of cancer-causing chemicals to the body. The consequences of its use fall into three general categories: cancer, and cardiovascular and respiratory disease. In the United States annually, *"Cigarette smoking causes about one of every five deaths"*. (1)

The apparent aim of the so-called 'War on Drugs' is to prevent and minimise harm to health and welfare due to the use of psychoactive substances. However, if this premise was to be applied equally and without exception, the suppliers and users of alcohol and tobacco would be criminalised and, therefore, subject to sanction from the criminal justice system for supplying and using drugs that pose a significant threat to health and welfare. This would be done to provide for punishment and deterrence in relation to supply and use of the substances.

Secondly, there is no evidence indicating that an overdose of heroin results in injury or death caused by compromise or cessation of breathing. If it was the case that an overdose of heroin was capable of causing harmful reduction or cessation of respiration there would be a significant and unequivocal body of evidence accumulated over a period of decades in support of this concept.

The portrayal of heroin as a substance capable of causing death due to respiratory failure resulting solely from the administration of an overdose is one that is made without supporting evidence.

Heroin is considered a pro-drug for morphine meaning it is, in essence, a delivery system for morphine. Heroin is metabolised rapidly to morphine once in the body. Opioid-agonist drugs such as morphine have no maximum dose meaning they can be administered until pain relief is achieved without regard to the total amount given: doses as large as 1,568 mg/h (milligrams per hour) morphine have been administered by continuous infusion. (2 p.103) They also have no ceiling effect meaning they do not reach a level in the body at which they cease to impart a therapeutic effect.

The evidence that does exist in relation to heroin and breathing is that significant overdose does not result in harm. In a modern clinical and controlled study, participants receiving high dose heroin-maintenance treatment administered significant overdoses of the drug with no harm resulting. (3)

Unaware of the magnitude of the dose they were receiving, study participants administered 67%, 100% and 150% of their usual dose. The maximum overdose given during the study was 150 mg and the largest single dose was 450 mg. As was noted in the study, *"Increments*

4

of 50% of the regular heroin dose did not cause any serious side effect." (3 p.86)

To summarise these findings, firstly, participants experiencing overdoses of up to 150 mg of heroin were not in any danger in relation to breathing or otherwise. If it was the case that an overdose of heroin was capable of causing harm it would have been immediately apparent during this study.

Secondly, the highest blood-morphine level recorded during the study was less than 1.5 mg/L. (3 p.90) This is a level entirely consistent with that found in people receiving morphine for the treatment of pain. This finding is extremely significant in light of the very large amounts of heroin administered. It illustrates the extraordinary capacity of the human body to metabolise the drug and, importantly, its primary active metabolite morphine. Even with massive and fluent intravenous injections of heroin nothing but therapeutic blood-morphine levels resulted. Doses taken by recreational users are typically a fraction of those given in the study.

Consistently, only very low levels of morphine are found in cases in which metabolites of heroin are present. In a study of *"Heroin-related deaths in New South Wales* [a state of Australia]*, 1992"*, *"the median blood-morphine level was 0.24 mg/L"* which is an extremely low level of the substance. (4 p.4)

5

The study unequivocally proves that there is no danger to breathing from substantial overdose of heroin and, accordingly, its primary active metabolite morphine.

As a further indication of morphine not being dangerous in relation to breathing, the substance is the accepted symptomatic treatment for shortness of breath in the palliative-care setting. Dyspnoea is a distressing feeling of difficulty in breathing. Morphine provides relief from the symptom of breathlessness without endangering the patient.

When opioids such as heroin are involved in drug-related deaths or adverse events related to breathing, the circumstance consistently encountered is the presence of combinations of central nervous system depressant drugs. The aforementioned study in which morphine was present in most subjects found that "*In 71%* [of subjects], *two or more different drugs were found at autopsy, and in 18% three or more drugs were detected.*" (4 p.4)

The combining of different classes of central nervous system depressant drugs can have a synergistic effect that results in sedation far in excess of that produced by any of the drugs in isolation. This profound sedation can lead to airway obstruction and asphyxiation (oxygen starvation). This situation can occur as a result of many combinations of substances that do not involve heroin or other opioids.

It is common with combinations of drugs including alcohol that vomit is the factor that causes or exacerbates airway obstruction. Alcohol is a uniquely dangerous drug in relation to contributing to compromised breathing and is commonly implicated in adverse events related to breathing that involve combinations of drugs.

The sequence of events in adverse incidents involving combinations of substances including opioids, dangerous sedation and breathing can be typified as follows. The person already has one or more central nervous system depressant drugs in their body such as alcohol, benzodiazepines or barbiturates, for example. They then take an opioid such as heroin. The combination of substances results in profound and disabling sedation with the person rendered unconscious and unable to be roused. The presence of two or more different classes of depressant drugs acting on similar or dissimilar classes of receptor in the brain can initiate a neurological process resulting in profound and dangerous sedation.

Due to being unconscious, the person is unable to maintain their airway and, consequently, becomes vulnerable to airway obstruction. Their head may fall forward, for example, resulting in impaired breathing due to structures in their throat impeding the flow of air to and from their lungs. If the person's breathing becomes impaired to the point that inadequate oxygen intake

7

occurs injury or death may result. This process is not related to cessation of the autonomic control of breathing: it is simply a physical restriction limiting or preventing the flow of air.

That heroin is not a uniquely dangerous drug is one of the most important pieces of information required to enable full understanding of the policy regime represented as a war on drugs.

So at this point, it is clear that the policy known as the 'War on Drugs' cannot be about preventing and minimising by way of punishment and deterrence the supply and use of drugs on the basis of the substances being a threat to health and welfare. Firstly, alcohol and tobacco are the two most dangerous drugs in existence yet the suppliers and users of these two substances (and caffeine) are not criminalised as part of a supposed response to drug-related harm. Associations with these substances are deemed lawful and, therefore, people do not commit an offence when engaged in possession, use, and lawful supply of the drugs.

There is only one way the so-called 'War on Drugs' could be genuine as a response to the use of psychoactive substances on the grounds of preventing and minimising harm to health and welfare. This is the criminalisation of associations (including supply, possession and use) with all drugs whose use has the capacity for harm including the two most dangerous drugs in existence (alcohol and tobacco) and caffeine.

Secondly, regarding the substances that the policy regime is supposedly a response to, the public portrayal by governments and their agencies of the drugs and their capacity for harm is not supported by evidence. In relation to heroin, there is not and never has been any evidence that it is capable of causing harmful compromise or cessation of breathing.

Therefore, regarding the psychoactive substances used by people, their respective dangers and the treatment by the criminal justice system of their suppliers and users, obvious inconsistencies and double standards exist.

THE BEHAVIOUR AND MECHANISMS BEHIND A POLICY REGIME

Before the true nature of the 'War on Drugs' is discussed, there is one fundamental point of interest that requires consideration along with an examination of the instrument in law that facilitates the imposition of legal sanctions upon people based on associations with particular psychoactive substances. Some other relevant concepts will also be discussed.

The fundamental point that firstly needs to be examined and acknowledged is the process that leads to people who are exhibiting the behaviour of using a drug of choice being categorised into two different groups which are treated in two very different ways.

We are aware that when it comes to so-called 'drug policy' there are two relevant categories of behaviour. The first is the behaviour of using the drugs alcohol, tobacco, and caffeine. This activity is deemed lawful and, therefore, not an offence even though two of these drugs are supremely dangerous and account for the vast majority of drug-related harm and mortality.

The second is the behaviour of using a drug other than alcohol, tobacco and caffeine. This behaviour is deemed unlawful and is therefore an offence. However, both behaviours are fundamentally the same. People are merely using their drug of choice. There is only one type of behaviour being exhibited whatever the substance and its capacity for harm. Drugs such as alcohol and tobacco are capable of profound harm while other substances are, in relative terms, far less harmful.

What then leads to the situation in which one type of behaviour (using a drug of choice) is subject to two very different sets of consequences in terms of the criminal justice system?

In relation to determining the consequences for those people who happen to use substances other than alcohol, tobacco and caffeine, there are two relevant points of interest relating to the political process. Both are fundamentally related to self-interest.

LAW MAKING AND SELF-INTEREST

Let's say that as a hypothetical scenario, a strategy is proposed to prevent and minimise the use of drugs as a means of protecting health and welfare. It is decided to use criminal sanctions to achieve these goals. Of course, the primary focus will be on the two most dangerous drugs in existence: alcohol and tobacco.

Laws are drafted that make supply, possession and use of these two drugs unlawful acts and, therefore, offences. An interesting point regarding self-interest is immediately apparent.

Let us assume that eighty percent of politicians use and enjoy alcohol. It is certain that no politician would support the formulation and enacting of laws that made possession and use of their drug of choice unlawful acts. They would vigorously oppose a situation in which they would be personally subject to criminal sanctions relating to use of the drug.

It is almost certain that the vast majority of their colleagues who do not use alcohol would also not support measures such as this. Obviously, a scenario such as this would not proceed past the conceptual stage.

Needless to say, if the supply, possession and use of alcohol, tobacco and caffeine was to be made unlawful and the laws duly enforced, society would be largely dysfunctional. As a conservative estimate, eighty percent of people would be engaging in unlawful behaviour on a daily basis. A situation such as this would not even be suggested as being plausible or desirable and would be prevented predominately by the principles of self-interest including that of political survival. Politicians almost without exception would react to the suggestion of such a scenario with mirth, derision and summary dismissal.

VOTING AND SELF-INTEREST

In a democracy, politicians are installed by the populace and ultimately are answerable to the populace. Would a politician in a democracy support the formulation and enacting of laws that made the drug-taking behaviour (in respect of alcohol, tobacco and caffeine) of the majority of the voting public and, therefore, the body of people that elect and subsequently employ them an unlawful act?

No, they would not. Voters would be disinclined to vote for a political party that made their drug-taking behaviour subject to criminal penalty. They would generally not vote for such a party due to self-interest. The mere suggestion of such a policy would result in its proponents being immediately relegated to a position of political irrelevance.

The processes of law making and electing those who formulate and enact the laws are ones that are, in relation to the 'War on Drugs', fundamentally and inextricably linked to and influenced by self-interest.

THE ESCALATION OF
AN INTERNATIONAL REGIME

President Richard Nixon is generally accepted as the figurehead of the modern day escalation of a policy regime portrayed as being protective in relation to health and welfare and that went on to be known as the 'War on

13

Drugs'. In a press conference in 1971, he announced that *"America's public enemy number one in the United States"* was *"drug abuse"* and that a *"new all out offensive"* would be waged upon the apparent threat. He solemnly conveyed that his administration would respond in a forthright manner to the allegedly grave problem and that the resources provided by his government would allow the U.S. to *"fight and defeat this enemy"*. (5)

However, his strategy notably omitted three drugs: alcohol and tobacco (the two most dangerous drugs in existence) and caffeine. The drug-taking behaviour of himself, his administration and its agents and the general populace in respect of the three most popular drugs was therefore exempt from the policy. This was in line with the Controlled Substances Act being signed into law during Nixon's tenure as president. The exclusion of the drugs alcohol, tobacco and caffeine gives full and obvious notice of the strategy having purposes other than the control of supply and use of psychoactive substances on the basis of protecting health and welfare.

He made a veiled and particularly ominous reference to opium use by mentioning *"the fact that a number of young Americans have become addicts as they serve abroad"*. (5) This reference made it clear that the supply and use of opium and its derivatives, in particular morphine, would continue to be criminalised and,

14

consequently, subject to legal sanction and enforcement activities.

There were, in particular, some equally ominous points made in the press conference in which President Nixon announced the details of the strategy that he repeatedly referred to as an 'offensive' and which was to be fuelled by substantial amounts of public money.

He emphasised that *"money will be provided to the extent that it is necessary"*. He made reference to $155 million in new funds he had requested from congress that would bring the total amount in the budget for *"drug abuse"* to *"over 350 million dollars"*. He announced that this money would be made available for the activities of *"enforcement and treatment"*. (5)

Obviously, he was eager for the distribution of substantial amounts of public money one year prior to a presidential election that he went on to win convincingly with a significant historical majority. As a politician well versed in the political advantage created by the distribution of public money, he set in train the allocation of money for enforcement and 'treatment' activities that was to increase regularly and substantially over subsequent decades.

President Nixon emphasised that the strategy would not apply solely to the United States. The *"worldwide offensive"* would also apply to *"the problems of sources of supply*" and so was ushered in an international regime enforced by the United States. (5) That the president unashamedly announced that the U.S. would impose the 'offensive' on the entire world was a chilling portent of the reach of the policy that would ultimately be administered by the United Nations.

He warned the American people that the 'danger' would not conclude with the ending of the Vietnam war and that the public must recognise the issue as an ongoing one. In essence, he announced a perpetual 'conflict' with no apparent endpoint therefore one requiring continual allocation of funds and ongoing commitment from government and its agents.

He also consolidated the government's nine separate agencies concerned with illicit drug matters by creating the overarching Special Action Office for Drug Abuse Prevention.

The world would enter a new age of cruelty and oppression from this point on and each subsequent president would augment the phenomenon with increases in funding and an unwavering commitment to its continuation. Effectively, the war in Vietnam was replaced by a 'conflict' based upon the criminalisation of people's behaviour in relation to the supply, possession and use of psychoactive substances other than alcohol, tobacco and caffeine.

The policy regime President Nixon reinforced had the characteristic of being endless and, therefore, possessed a unique political utility which has seen it continue unhindered to this day.

THE DOUBLE STANDARD

Let's focus on what might be called the 'behavioural double standard'. We have discussed how politicians would not be involved in the formulation of legislation that would be harmful to themselves or the majority in society. They would never permit legislation that would criminalise themselves or the majority of the voting public in relation to the use of a drug of choice when that drug is alcohol, tobacco or caffeine.

To criminalise themselves would be personally detrimental and to criminalise the majority of the voting public as defined by their personal drug use would constitute a politically unfeasible act. Such actions would also be untenable in terms of the functioning and fundamental viability of society.

But as history has shown, politicians and the majority in society have had an uncommon enthusiasm for engaging in and supporting the criminalising of a minority as defined by their drug use in order to facilitate financial and political gain. This is the double standard in terms of the 'War on Drugs' that currently draws most attention from those with a cursory interest in the subject. It also leads one back to the fundamental question: why are some people committing an offence in respect of drug-related behaviours when others are not?

Ultimately though, the double standard displayed in relation to the use of psychoactive substances and the treatment of suppliers and users is not explained by anything related to the actual use of or harm caused by substances. It is explained by the process of defining and subsequently utilising a minority in order to achieve financial gain and political advantage.

CONTROLLED SUBSTANCES: THE CREATION OF CRIME

The purpose of the Controlled Substances Act (U.S.) and its international equivalents is portrayed as being the categorisation of substances whose use has the capacity to be harmful to health and welfare. Associations with substances determined to be controlled are deemed unlawful apparently on the basis of preventing and minimising supply and use of the drugs in order to protect the health and welfare of people.

However, as is the case with the 'drug-related' treaties administered by the United Nations and upon which it is based, three drugs are excluded from the Act and its international equivalents. Alcohol, tobacco and caffeine are not deemed controlled substances and, therefore, associations with them are lawful and not subject to criminal sanctions.

The following statement makes reference to two of the exemptions in the Controlled Substances Act and, thereby, lays bare the profoundly and fundamentally duplicitous nature of the Act and any law based upon it.

> *"There are also a number of substances that are abused but not regulated under the CSA* [Controlled Substances Act]. *Alcohol and tobacco, for example, are specifically exempt from control by the CSA."*
>
> Drug Enforcement Administration (6 p.47)

Obviously, the categorisation of substances in the document is not genuine regarding a response to the supply and possession of drugs whose use has the capacity to be harmful to health and welfare. Obviously, the purpose of the Act cannot be related to addressing harm to health and welfare resulting from the use of psychoactive substances.

The Controlled Substances Act and its international equivalents are solely mechanisms of selective crime creation. The Act categorises the substances with which an association is unlawful solely for the purpose of defining and creating a resource of people that is utilised in order to enable financial gain and political advantage.

Activities of supply and possession involving substances defined in the Act are deemed offences not because of any desire for the protection of health and welfare in relation to use of the substances.

Associations with the drugs alcohol, tobacco and caffeine are not subject to criminalisation due to these substances not being included in the Act. Accordingly, people engaged in possession, use, and lawful supply of these drugs of choice are not defined as being subject to criminalisation. The Controlled Substances Act and its international equivalents selectively create and maintain crime upon which two fundamental categories of economic enterprise are based.

THE SUPPLY OF DRUGS OTHER THAN ALCOHOL, TOBACCO AND CAFFEINE

The criminalisation of the supply of drugs other than alcohol, tobacco and caffeine creates a worldwide black market worth hundreds of billions of dollars annually and which therefore comprises an economic system of significant consequence.

THE POSSESSION OF DRUGS OTHER THAN ALCOHOL, TOBACCO AND CAFFEINE

The criminalisation of possession of drugs other than alcohol, tobacco and caffeine creates a criminal underclass that forms the basis for a worldwide industry of enforcement activities including arrest, imprisonment and other endeavours which are funded by public money and sustain a large number of people and organisations.

Obvious proof cf the fraudulent nature of the Controlled Substances Act is the classification of heroin. Heroin is a valuable way of administering morphine as it undergoes a rapid but gradual transformation to the substance once in the body. Heroin was widely utilised in medicine in many parts of the world before the U.S. agitated for its use to become prohibited for medical and non-medical purposes. It remains in use in the United Kingdom for the treatment of severe acute pain in the hospital emergency setting.

In the Controlled Substances Act, the substance is classified in Schedule 1. Substances in this classification are deemed to have "*no currently accepted medical use in treatment in the United States.*" (6 p.9) However, the drug has always had and continues to have a valuable and accepted medical use. The U.S. chooses to ignore and deny this fact as part of their ongoing desire to have the supply and possession of heroin criminalised on an international level.

In the early 1950s, the U.S. lobbied for the cessation of the medical use of heroin globally through the World Health Organisation regardless of its valuable utility. They submitted a draft resolution in which they recommended that *"campaigns be undertaken with the assistance of appropriate bodies to convince doctors and governments that diacetylmorphine is not a drug of necessity for medical practice"* and that *"member States which have not already done so abolish the importation and production of diacetylmorphine."* (7 p.2)

For the purpose of controlling the availability of heroin, the almost complete cessation of medical use of a valuable drug on a worldwide basis was achieved. In doing so, the U.S. apparently had little concern regarding their own citizens being deprived of its use.

A SUCCESSFUL POLITICAL STRATEGY: THE CREATION OF FEAR

An age-old way to garner support for a political strategy is to create the perception of a threat and then appear to protect the populace from the perceived threat. The illusion of an enemy can be created to provide justification for a conflict or endeavour that brings with it economic activity and, therefore, financial gain and political advantage.

President Nixon achieved this with great effectiveness in 1971 when he announced that *"public enemy number one"* was *"drug abuse"*. (5) He claimed that use of drugs other than alcohol, tobacco and caffeine was the predominant threat to the American people in relation to health and welfare. He created the illusion of a threat to survival and very effectively instilled fear in the people. He then asserted that he would seek to protect the populace by waging an 'offensive' against the threat thereby keeping it at bay and minimising any chance that it may harm people.

As has previously been noted, the apparent protection of the populace from an alleged threat to their health and welfare was obviously a very successful political strategy. The fact that the threat was contrived and that the 'offensive' actually had entirely different motivations would not have been appreciated by the vast majority of people.

THE TERMINOLOGY OF FEAR
AND HOSTILITY

A fundamental instrument of propaganda utilised as part of the 'War on Drugs' is use of the word 'drug'. The term is used almost exclusively in reference to substances other than alcohol, tobacco and caffeine. The drugs of the majority (alcohol, tobacco and caffeine) are generally not referred to as being 'drugs' even though they are indeed 'drugs' and, in respect of alcohol and tobacco, substances whose use results in substantial harm, mortality and immense healthcare-related and associated costs being imposed upon society.

The word 'drug' through its association with a minority is given a negative connotation. A false and self-serving distinction is thereby made: that alcohol, tobacco and caffeine are not 'drugs' and, therefore, are somehow a lesser threat to health and welfare.

This incorrect semantic distinction allows the majority to believe that their drug-taking behaviour in respect of alcohol, tobacco and caffeine is not what it actually is: which is drug-taking behaviour. This act of denial (refusing to acknowledge what is obviously the case) allows the majority to justify and ignore the mistreatment of those defined by their use of other drugs.

Often used in combination with 'drug' is 'abuse'. 'Drug abuse' is a term almost exclusively used in reference to the use of drugs other than alcohol, tobacco and caffeine. The term implies that use of such substances is an act that is somehow deviant, inherently self-destructive and different in nature to use of the three licit drugs. However, the use of other drugs entails exactly the same fundamental psychological processes as does the use of alcohol, tobacco and caffeine.

The term 'drug abuse' is rarely applied to the use of alcohol, tobacco and caffeine. The use of these drugs is portrayed as being completely normal, socially acceptable and a basic right that any adult can and should be able to exercise.

Without doubt, the term used with the most venom to compartmentalise those who use drugs other than alcohol, tobacco and caffeine is 'addict'. The term is used in an aggressive and wholly pejorative manner, in particular, to describe those who use opioids. It is used to convey hostility towards a minority and often in concert with blatant hypocrisy as many of those who use the term are physically dependent on a substance themselves.

The term is used by some to imply that the use of opioids inherently results in a chaotic lifestyle and the circumstances arising from this. However, the actual cause of the majority of misfortune is consequences of the criminalisation and subsequent oppression of users: conditions enforced upon them by the state.

The term is also used to imply that users of illicit substances who have chaotic lives due to being criminalised as defined by their substance use have somehow brought the consequences of the criminalisation upon themselves by way of their personal choices. This provides a convenient way for those who vote for and support the laws that result in the criminalisation to deny any personal responsibility and, therefore, complicity in the situation.

The insinuation that only those who use drugs other than alcohol, tobacco and caffeine are susceptible to physical dependency and compulsive drug-taking behaviour and, therefore, the title of 'addict' is indicative of the ubiquitous nature of hostility and hypocrisy when references to others are made under the banner of psychoactive substance use. This hostility is continually played out and reinforced in the media in all its forms and is unique in terms of its vigour and persistence.

THE WAR ON DRUGS IS NOT PROHIBITION

The policy regime known as the 'War on Drugs' is commonly referred to as 'prohibition' which was the term given to the alcohol control policy in place in the United States from 1920 to 1933. There is, however, one fundamental difference between the two policies that unequivocally invalidates use of the term 'prohibition' to draw parallels with the modern phenomenon known as the 'War on Drugs'.

Under U.S. federal prohibition, possession relating to personal use of alcohol was not specifically subject to criminal sanctions. The amendment stated that *"the manufacture, sale, or transportation of intoxicating liquors within, the importation thereof into, or the exportation thereof from the United States and all territory subject to the jurisdiction thereof for beverage purposes is hereby prohibited."* (8) There is no reference in the amendment to possession of alcohol being subject to criminal sanctions when the sole intention of possession is use of the substance.

The so-called 'War on Drugs' is fundamentally different to 'prohibition' because it involves the criminalisation of possession of a substance when that possession is related solely to use. Whereas alcohol prohibition was in part an intervention to prevent some of the unfortunate consequences of alcohol use such as its contribution to domestic violence, the 'War on Drugs' has a singular aim to criminalise and, subsequently, utilise people for purposes unrelated to a response to any harm caused by psychoactive substance use.

SUMMARY

A summary of fundamentally important points so far:

- The so-called 'War on Drugs' is not concerned in any way with preventing the supply and use of drugs that present a threat to health and welfare. If the purpose of the 'War on Drugs' was to control the supply and use of drugs on the basis of the use of substances being a threat to health and welfare, the supply and use of alcohol and tobacco would be its primary focus. Associations with the two most dangerous drugs in existence (alcohol and tobacco) and caffeine are not addressed by the policy.

The only way the Controlled Substances Act and its international equivalents could be genuine in relation to the prevention and minimisation of drug-related harm would be the inclusion of alcohol, tobacco and caffeine in the documents and, thereby, the criminalisation of supply, possession and use of all psychoactive substances with a capacity for harm to health and welfare.

- The fundamental mechanism in law underpinning the policy regime is the criminalisation of a minority. The minority is defined solely by their associations with drugs other than alcohol, tobacco and caffeine. The defining of people for criminalisation is carried out in the Controlled Substances Act (U.S.) and its international equivalents.

- The two most dangerous drugs in existence (alcohol and tobacco) and caffeine are the drugs of the majority including, importantly, those who profit from the criminalisation and exploitation of a minority as defined by their substance use. Drugs other than alcohol, tobacco and caffeine are the drugs of a minority of people.

- In generalised terms, current 'drug policy' or the 'War on Drugs' is portrayed as a policy device, in particular, to prevent and minimise the use of heroin. The long-standing myth is that injury or death may occur if 'too much' (an overdose) is taken due to the effects of morphine on breathing. The concept is, however, without supporting evidence. Heroin is proven not to be dangerous even in substantial overdose.

THE TRUE NATURE OF THE
WAR ON DRUGS: AN
ECONOMIC SYSTEM BASED ON
INTENTIONALLY-CREATED CRIME

The so-called 'War on Drugs' is not concerned with addressing harm related to the use of psychoactive substances of any kind. If its purpose was to prevent and minimise harm due to the use of psychoactive substances it would address supply and use of the two most dangerous drugs in existence: alcohol and tobacco. Supply and use of these two drugs and caffeine is not addressed by the policy.

Obviously, the policy has intentions other than the prevention and minimisation of harm due to drug use. The actual intention is simply to create political advantage through two fundamental mechanisms.

Firstly, the allocation of public money to respond to a contrived problem. This amounts to tens of billions of dollars annually in the U.S. alone. The problem is portrayed as the consumption of drugs other than alcohol, tobacco and caffeine. The response is enforcement activities such as arrest, legal processing, fining, imprisoning and mandated interventions described as treatment. These activities constitute a worldwide industry that employs a large number of people in the public and private sectors.

Secondly, the creation and maintenance of a lucrative worldwide black market in substances other than alcohol, tobacco and caffeine. This enterprise generates hundreds of billions of dollars annually worldwide.

The enabling mechanism of the phenomenon is the intentional creation of crime via the criminalisation of associations with drugs other than alcohol, tobacco and caffeine. The categorisation of substances with which an association is criminalised is carried out in the Controlled Substances Act (U.S.) and its international equivalents. The intentional creation of crime and, consequently, criminals creates a resource of people that is utilised on an economic basis in order to enable financial gain and political advantage.

In order for the strategy to be politically achievable, the resource of people who are criminalised and, subsequently, economically utilised must be a minority. The creation of the minority is achieved simply by the criminalisation of associations with drugs other than alcohol, tobacco and caffeine.

The so-called 'War on Drugs' is simply a world-wide economic system based upon intentionally-created crime. It is an aggressive and unrelenting exploitation of a minority built upon a foundation of deception, hostility and hypocrisy.

To reiterate, the 'War on Drugs' is not concerned in any way with addressing drug-related harm: it is simply an economic system utilising a criminalised minority as the resource to be exploited. The criminalised minority is defined and, thereby, created solely by their associations via supply and possession with drugs other than alcohol, tobacco and caffeine. Again, it must be emphasised, the 'War on Drugs' is not concerned in any way with preventing or minimising drug-related harm.

A CONCISE DESCRIPTION

Following is an all-encompassing description, point by point, and in as concise terms as possible of the true nature of the so-called 'War on Drugs'.

The apparent purpose of the 'War on Drugs' is as a response to harm brought about by the use of psychoactive substances. Criminal sanctions are utilised as apparent methods of punishment and deterrence.

This rationale is obviously false, however, as associations with the two most dangerous drugs (alcohol and tobacco) and caffeine are not criminalised as are associations with other drugs. Obviously, the purpose of the policy is not related to the prevention and minimisation of drug-related harm.

The defining characteristic of the phenomenon is the intentional and selective creation of crime via the criminalisation of people's behaviour in relation to drugs other than alcohol, tobacco and caffeine. This categorisation of substances and, therefore, people's behaviour is carried out in the Controlled Substances Act (U.S.) and its international equivalents. The Act and its equivalents are based upon the 'drug-related' treaties administered by the United Nations.

The criminalisation of people who associate with substances other than alcohol, tobacco and caffeine is not related to any potential threat to their health and welfare. An association with the substances merely defines them as being subject to criminalisation purely for the purpose of creating a resource of people that is able to be utilised on an economic basis.

The use of associations with certain substances to define criminal behaviour allows for a minority to be criminalised and crime to be created under the guise of the protection of health and welfare.

Behaviours involving the drugs alcohol, tobacco and caffeine are not criminalised as doing so would criminalise a large proportion of the population including those who profit politically and financially from the crime created by the criminalisation of a minority.

The 'War on Drugs' is fundamentally a crime-creation and maintenance scheme based upon the criminalisation of a minority. The minority is defined for criminalisation solely by their associations with drugs other than alcohol, tobacco and caffeine.

It is a policy that delivers political advantage through the allocation of vast amounts of public money to address the contrived crime and financial benefit from the black market in drugs other than alcohol, tobacco and caffeine. It is simply a worldwide economic system based upon intentionally-created crime.

The only way the so-called 'War on Drugs' could not be a selective crime-creation and maintenance scheme is the categorisation of all drugs together (including alcohol, tobacco and caffeine) and them being subject to the same regulatory regime with no exceptions.

The 'War on Drugs' has not failed. It is in terms of its true motives an outstanding success: political advantage resulting from employment and profits enabled by the distribution of vast sums of public money and the existence of a lucrative worldwide black market in drugs other than alcohol, tobacco and caffeine. This is why it continues.

———————

THE ECONOMIC RESOURCE

The people comprising the economic resource are defined by associations with drugs other than alcohol, tobacco and caffeine. As a means of deceptively justifying the criminalisation of a minority, their association with the substances is portrayed as being uniquely harmful to them therefore apparently requiring the use of oppressive measures to protect them from their own behaviour.

In order to enable and sustain vast economic systems these people are able by law to be arrested, legally processed, fined, imprisoned and 'treated' solely on the basis of their associations with drugs other than alcohol, tobacco and caffeine. They are denied a legal and regulated supply of their drugs of choice obligating them to obtain the substances from and, thereby, sustain a highly profitable black market.

The Controlled Substances Act in the U.S. and its international equivalents are the instruments in law that provide for the criminalisation of the minority. The documents classify the substances with which an association is criminalised. Alcohol, tobacco and caffeine are excluded from the documents because the suppliers and users of these three substances are the majority in society and are therefore not subject to criminalisation and exploitation under the policy.

This selective criminalisation creates a class of people that is lawfully able to be used as an economic resource and whose treatment enables financial and political gain. This occurs simply because they are a minority and it is therefore politically achievable to impose upon them things that would never be imposed upon the law-makers, their agents and the majority of the population.

Of course, the ironic and defining double standard inherent in the phenomenon is that the drug-taking behaviour (in respect of alcohol, tobacco and caffeine) of those who make the laws and those who carry out the arresting, legal processing, fining, imprisoning and 'treatment' etc., is not subject to criminal sanctions.

Again, the 'War on Drugs' is not concerned in any way with the nature of any substance or its capacity for harm: substance use is merely a convenient way of defining those who comprise the economic resource to be exploited for financial gain and political advantage.

THE DRUGS THEMSELVES

In the 'War on Drugs', substances other than alcohol, tobacco and caffeine play two fundamental roles. Firstly, associations with the drugs provides a way of defining those who are to be economically utilised. Drug use itself cannot be used as a way of defining those who are to be arrested, fined, imprisoned, 'treated' or have their assets seized etc., as the vast majority of people in society use one or more of the drugs alcohol, tobacco and caffeine.

Therefore, the strategy used to define those who are to be exploited is the type of drug used. Opioid users are the obvious example. A very small number of people use opioids due to their unpleasant side effects: nausea and constipation. These people are portrayed as an undesirable segment of society due to them engaging in what is falsely characterised as a uniquely dangerous and unacceptable behaviour: use of a drug other than alcohol, tobacco and caffeine.

Due to them comprising a minority in society it is possible to alienate and utilise them for cynical political and economic purposes. It is politically achievable to treat a minority in a way that the majority would not accept being treated themselves.

Secondly, an enemy to be feared is created: in this case, drugs other than alcohol, tobacco and caffeine. In reality, alcohol and tobacco are the most dangerous drugs by far and in terms of drug-related harm these are the drugs of most concern. However, to create the illusion of an enemy, drugs other than alcohol, tobacco and caffeine are falsely portrayed as being uniquely dangerous and therefore to be feared. In addition to this falsehood is the fact that the substances themselves are inanimate objects and no-one is obligated to use them.

Human nature therefore dictates that the 'enemy' status of the substances is imposed on the users who are ostracised, scapegoated and mistreated merely because of an association with the drugs. The users of drugs other than alcohol, tobacco and caffeine are subject to hostility due purely to the fact that they associate with substances that the majority have been led to believe pose a unique threat to health and welfare.

The hostility of many towards the users of drugs other than alcohol, tobacco and caffeine is omnipresent in society and this is indicative of the capacity of human beings to be hostile towards one another given a convenient basis for the behaviour. Many of those for whom alcohol, tobacco, and caffeine use is a completely normal activity show no reluctance in meting out patronising and judgemental behaviour towards those who use different drugs.

Demand for psychoactive substances will never cease as the subjectively positive effects guarantee a committed desire by many to engage in use. The fact that substance use is a desirable behaviour for the majority in society delivers certainty for the economic activity created by the 'War on Drugs'. The policy regime fundamentally relies upon people having a desire for whatever reason to repeatedly seek out and consume psychoactive substances for their effects.

DENIAL OF REGULATED
MANUFACTURE

As has been detailed, the fundamental mechanism enabling what is represented as a war on drugs is the intentional creation of crime in order to facilitate financial gain and political advantage. This is achieved by the defining of a minority for criminalisation by the Controlled Substances Act (U.S.) and its international equivalents. There is also a circumstance resulting from the intentional creation of crime that requires discussion.

Supply of the two most dangerous drugs in existence (alcohol and tobacco) and caffeine is regulated to provide surety to consumers that the substances are manufactured to appropriate standards. Using alcohol as an example, its manufacture is controlled so as to ensure that ethanol is the sole alcohol contained in the product and that the concentration is known by the user. Regulation of alcohol manufacture is particularly important because the presence of methanol can lead to severe health-related consequences for the user.

As a consequence of the criminalisation of the supply of drugs other than alcohol, tobacco and caffeine, the regulation of these substances for consumer protection is denied to those who use them. Accordingly, the aggressive oppression of a minority manifests as two general circumstances. Firstly, they are criminalised in relation to possession and use of the substances in order to enable their utilisation on an economic basis. Secondly, they are forced to acquire the drugs from a black market. This denies them consumer protections in relation to manufacture of the substances that are afforded to the users of alcohol, tobacco, and caffeine.

COMPLIANCE AND ADMINISTRATION

Although the overall strategy originated in the U.S., administration of the three 'drug control' treaties and, therefore, the 'War on Drugs' is officially carried out by the United Nations. The overarching body charged with administration of the conventions is the United Nations Office on Drugs and Crime. The United Nations Commission on Narcotic Drugs is the *"policymaking body of the United Nations system with prime responsibility for drug-related matters."* (9)

The three conventions are the Single Convention on Narcotic Drugs of 1961 as amended by the 1972 Protocol, the Convention on Psychotropic Substances of 1971 and the United Nations Convention against Illicit Traffic in Narcotic Drugs and Psychotropic Substances of 1988. Countries entering into the treaties and, thereby, participating in the 'War on Drugs' are obliged to criminalise their citizens who associate on a non-authorised basis with the substances listed in the schedules contained in the documents.

The World Health Organisation (WHO) and the International Narcotics Control Board (INCB) are involved in the process of adding substances to or rescheduling substances already included in the drug scheduling system. As stated in a video explaining the scheduling process, *"the commission* [on narcotic drugs] *takes its scheduling decisions based on the scientific recommendations by WHO and INCB".* (10)

There are three fundamental objectives for those administering the scheduling system in order to maintain the policy regime that is represented as a war on drugs on either an overarching international or country-specific level. Firstly, maintenance of the scheduling of currently scheduled substances and, thereby, continuance of the situation in which associations with them constitute an offence. Secondly, that effectively every new psychoactive substance is added to the schedules. Finally, that alcohol, tobacco and caffeine are never scheduled and, therefore, associations with these three substances in relation to possession, use and lawful supply activities are never deemed an offence.

When reading through literature of the United Nations in relation to psychoactive substance use some familiar terms are encountered: 'drug policy', 'drug users' and

41

'drug abuse'. These terms are associated with four false concepts. Firstly, that the policy regime administered by the U.N. is a response to the use of psychoactive substances due to it causing harm to health and welfare. This is incorrect as the supply, possession and use of the drugs alcohol, tobacco and caffeine is not addressed by the mechanisms administered by the organisation.

Secondly, that the substances alcohol, tobacco and caffeine are not 'drugs' and, therefore, the behaviours associated with them are not deserving of oppressive mechanisms of control apparently on the basis of protecting health and welfare. This is incorrect as alcohol, tobacco and caffeine are substances taken voluntarily for their effects on the central nervous system in a non-medical context and are indeed, therefore, drugs.

Thirdly, that a 'drug user' is solely a person who uses substances other than alcohol, tobacco and caffeine and this simple association makes them deserving of treatment that would never be imposed upon users of the three popular drugs. This is incorrect as those who use alcohol, tobacco, and caffeine are indeed using drugs for the same fundamental reasons as those who use other drugs and are, therefore, 'drug users'.

Finally, that use of drugs other than alcohol, tobacco and caffeine is an improper, deviant and criminal act of using a substance for its effects on the central nervous system and is therefore a behaviour that must be discouraged and punished by the imposition of oppressive control measures including arrest, fines, imprisonment and mandated 'treatment'. This is incorrect as the use of other drugs constitutes exactly the same fundamental activity as is involved in use of the drugs alcohol, tobacco and caffeine and is, therefore, not a less valid or more morally questionable behaviour.

The term used by the United Nations to describe the issue they are apparently responding to is the 'world drug problem'. However, the 'world drug problem' is by definition a phenomenon that does not involve harm caused to health and welfare by supply and use of the drugs alcohol, tobacco and caffeine.

Accordingly, the United Nations is therefore apparently concerned about the use of drugs on the basis of its capacity to cause harm but is not concerned about supply and use of the two most dangerous drugs in existence (alcohol and tobacco) and caffeine. It does not seek therefore to be involved in the regulation of associations with these three drugs by way of measures including the criminalisation of supply and possession in order to prevent and minimise harm to the health and welfare of people.

The schedules contained in the Single Convention on Narcotic Drugs, 1961, as amended by the 1972 Protocol and the Convention on Psychotropic Substances of 1971 list the substances controlled for reasons apparently related to the protection of health and welfare.

The fundamental circumstance that illustrates the duplicitous nature of the entire United Nations system that is portrayed as existing to address the use of drugs on the grounds of health and welfare is that the two most dangerous drugs in existence (alcohol and tobacco) and caffeine are not listed in the schedules. Accordingly, associations with them are not subject to control and, therefore, the imposition of criminal sanctions.

Fundamentally, the United Nations formulates, administers and maintains an international system of conventions that provides the foundation for the criminalisation of the suppliers and users of drugs other than alcohol, tobacco and caffeine. This policy facilitates substantial financial gain and political advantage.

The three United Nations 'drug control' conventions are the fundamental basis for a worldwide regime of enforcement activities responding to intentionally-created crime. These activities employ a large number of people, are funded by public money and constitute an industry of significant proportions. This enterprise manifests as the aggressive and unrelenting economic utilisation of a minority who are criminalised solely for the purpose of enabling the exploitation.

AN ACCURATE TERM

The term 'War on Drugs' has been used for half a century to imply that the strategy is one that seeks to prevent and minimise the supply and use of psychoactive substances on the basis of preventing and minimising harm to health and welfare. As has been discussed, this is entirely a deception as supply and use of the two most dangerous drugs in existence (alcohol and tobacco) and caffeine is not addressed by the policy.

Having determined that the 'War on Drugs' is not related to the prevention and minimisation of drug-related harm and is actually a worldwide economic system based upon intentionally-created crime facilitated by the criminalisation of a minority, an appropriate term must be used that accurately describes its true nature. The use of a wholly inaccurate and deceptive term ('War on Drugs') is not appropriate and is counterproductive in relation to a worthwhile discussion taking place regarding a policy that actually relies upon the supply and use of psychoactive substances other than alcohol, tobacco and caffeine.

The acronym that will be used from this point on to refer to the phenomenon is one that represents its nature accurately and assists in a genuine conversation and analysis of the situation taking place.

GESICC

Global Economic System based on
Intentionally-Created Crime

———————

THE MONEY, WHERE IT COMES FROM AND WHO BENEFITS

MONEY FROM THE BLACK MARKET

It is basic economic theory that if demand for a product exists and supply is restricted, the price increases accordingly. In relation to psychoactive substances, the principle is equally relevant. Demand for drugs of any kind will remain strong regardless of any controls placed upon their supply.

It is well established that when the supply of psychoactive substances is restricted there are those who will engage in supply activities to meet demand regardless of legal sanctions being in place. This situation occurred during alcohol prohibition and led to the involvement of organised crime in supply of the substance due to large, tax-free profits being available.

A 2014 report estimated the amount spent on cannabis, cocaine, heroin and methamphetamine annually in the U.S. alone to be *"on the order of $100 billion"*. (11 p.2) As far as the worldwide trade in illicit drugs of all kinds, it is estimated that the annual figure for the global black market in these substances to be in the region of at least four hundred billion dollars.

WHO BENEFITS FROM THE
BLACK MARKET?

Beneficiaries of the black market in drugs other than alcohol, tobacco and caffeine might be broadly categorised into two groups. Firstly, those who are prepared to risk criminal penalties including imprisonment and even execution to profit from the supply of substances. The endeavour can be lucrative with substantial tax-free profits possible but obviously, for some, it can entail substantial risks. There are always those who will accept the inherent risks to engage in such an enterprise.

If we remove the double standard, what is the fundamental difference between a supplier of alcohol and a supplier of opioids? Absolutely nothing. Both parties are supplying a central nervous system depressant drug that people take voluntarily for its effects. One (alcohol) is far more dangerous than the other (opioids) but they are both drugs of choice taken by people for their subjectively positive psychoactive effects.

Secondly, those who form part of the legitimate economy but who benefit from the money that the illegitimate or black economy produces. The black market in illicit substances generates enormous profits and a significant amount of this money is subject to laundering processes and, consequently, becomes legitimate capital. The process of transforming money created by criminal enterprise into money deemed as being legitimately acquired is complex and can involve various parts of the financial services industry.

The worldwide black market in illicit drugs constitutes an economy of substantial proportions. Those who benefit from this massive tax-free cash economy would be highly supportive of efforts to maintain the existence of the GESICC.

Obviously, many people and various entities benefit directly or indirectly from the existence of the black market in drugs other than alcohol, tobacco and caffeine. It has been intentionally maintained for many decades and, therefore, its persistence can only be evidence of its advantageous and desirable nature in relation to various and diverse people and entities.

MONEY DERIVED FROM GOVERNMENT

Regarding money derived from government, the GESICC is quite simply an extremely successful mechanism for enabling the distribution of public money. The expenditure is justified as being required to address the supply and use of drugs other than alcohol, tobacco and caffeine on the basis of it being a threat to health and welfare. This specious justification provides the basis upon which public money is distributed to various sectors of the economy with enforcement agencies being the predominant beneficiaries. The expenditure is generally incorrectly perceived by the public as being necessary for the protection of their health and welfare and is therefore largely unopposed and unquestioned.

The distribution of public money brings with it political advantage as the recipients of the money are supportive of the administrations and individual politicians that allocated the funds. This in turn manifests as support at the ballot box with the companies, their employees and other beneficiaries voting for and donating to the political parties that distributed the money. There is possibly no more efficient way of eliciting support from the voting public than the distribution of money that enables employment and profits and, consequently, people's financial security.

ALLOCATION OF PUBLIC MONEY

Since the industrial revolution and the advent of mechanisation, there has been a substantial reduction in the amount of manual labour required to produce goods and services. With increasing population and decreasing demand for manual labour, a way of supporting those who were deemed surplus to an economy's requirements was needed to prevent a continuing situation of substantial unemployment and, as a result of this, some degree of humanitarian crisis. Consequently, welfare was introduced. In applicable societies, the government assists monetarily those who cannot support themselves via employment or some other form of economic enterprise.

In many societies, however, the distribution of welfare can be dishonest and selective. Welfare to the poor and unemployed is generally portrayed as being a financial liability and, therefore, to be minimised whilst, at the same time, money is generously distributed to others under the guise of an accommodating strategy. These strategies are used to justify the distribution of money in the public eye by providing apparent grounds for the allocation of funds. One of these strategies is, unfortunately, war. Hence the 'War on Drugs'.

Australia spends a substantial amount of money per annum on enforcement of so-called 'drug policy'. What does this mean? It simply means that a number of Australians are employed to hunt down fellow human beings and forcibly involve them in the criminal justice system. It is to be noted that many of those involved in the arresting, legal processing, fining and imprisoning of others apparently on the basis of a behaviour involving possession and use of a psychoactive substance exhibit exactly the same behaviour involving the drugs alcohol, tobacco, and caffeine.

The justification given for this treatment of a minority is that it is a measure required for the protection of health and welfare. The actual purpose of the policy is financial gain and the political advantage this enables. An astonishing amount of money is devoted to the GESICC each year in the United States with a total of *"$44.5 billion"* requested *"for National Drug Control Program agencies* [Fiscal Year 2025 Budget]". (12) A considerable sum is also spent by the states with the total amount distributed possibly exceeding $50 billion annually.

WHO BENEFITS FROM PUBLIC MONEY?

The number and nature of organisations and people that benefit from the money distributed under the banner of the GESICC is significant and varied. The following is a brief account of some of the recipients of public money.

LAW ENFORCEMENT

The obvious example is the Drug Enforcement Administration in the United States which is concerned with enforcing laws related to supply. It is part of the Department of Justice and employs *"more than 9200 men and women*". (13) In 2020, DEA agents carried out 26,264 arrests classed as 'domestic'. (14) It had an annual budget for the fiscal year 2021 of $3.28 billion. (15) The organisation has an international presence with "*86 offices in 67 countries around the world* [2015]". (13)

Imagine a world in which there is a dedicated organisation whose sole purpose is to forcibly involve in the criminal justice system people who choose to be involved in the supply of alcohol, tobacco, and caffeine. Obviously, apart from being untenable in terms of the functioning of society it would rightfully be identified as a human-rights abuse regardless of the justification offered. This situation is, however, being imposed upon those choosing to be involved in the supply of drugs other than alcohol, tobacco and caffeine.

Worldwide, law enforcement organisations and various other entities are involved in unequivocally inequitable conduct whilst enforcing so-called 'drug laws'. Their work has them forcibly involving in the criminal justice system those defined solely by their associations with psychoactive substances other than alcohol, tobacco and caffeine. This activity is for no other reason than for economic and political purposes. The enforcement sector has considerable political influence and traditionally has been the major recipient of public money distributed as part of the GESICC.

THE PRISON INDUSTRY

In the U.S. in 2022, approximately 66,000 people were in federal prisons due to drug-related offences. This was 46% of all prisoners. (16 p.33) The average sentence duration for 'drug' offenders in federal prisons has been in excess of ten years. (17 p.14) Categorised on the basis of race, 71% of federal prisoners serving drug-related sentences were Black or Hispanic (Sept. 30, 2022). (16 p.33) In state-run prisons in 2022, 24.6% of female prisoners (17,036 persons) and 11.6% of male prisoners (110,436 persons) were sentenced for 'drug' offences according to U.S. Department of Justice statistics. (16 p.29)

This is a staggering total of approximately 193,400 people imprisoned in one country alone, in two prison systems, apparently on the basis of punishing them due to them having associated with a drug other than alcohol, tobacco and caffeine. But the association with the particular drugs only serves as the false justification for involving a minority in the criminal justice system purely for the purpose of enabling economic and political gain.

The mass imprisonment of these people is a lucrative industry funded by public money and is perhaps the most obvious atrocity associated with the GESICC. There is possibly no greater indication of the capacity of people to act in a mercenary nature than the imprisonment of their fellow man purely for financial gain.

THE LEGAL PROFESSION

The GESICC provides substantial opportunity for many in the legal profession particularly in relation to the representation of those arrested and charged due to involvement in supply or possession of drugs other than alcohol, tobacco and caffeine.

ACADEMIA

There are entire departments within some tertiary education facilities devoted solely to study of the GESICC. Every imaginable facet of the situation is the subject of endless study and analysis which is largely not for any actual reason other than to provide the basis for employment of academic and support staff. The oppression of people provides a rich and perpetual source of material to form the basis for academic research and inquiry.

WELFARE AND ADVOCACY

The welfare and advocacy sectors are predominantly funded by government and a proportion of the people they assist are subject to the negative affects of being criminalised and economically utilised as defined by associations with drugs other than alcohol, tobacco and caffeine. The welfare and advocacy organisations providing services to those affected are served well by the lives of these people being made chaotic by the selective criminalisation utilised by the GESICC as this situation provides them with a perpetual client base consisting of oppressed and disenfranchised people.

TREATMENT

The mandated 'treatment' of people from the court system is now a lucrative industry in the U.S. and elsewhere. The circumstance that leads to people being forced into 'treatment' is simply possession of a drug other than alcohol, tobacco and caffeine. The sector is guaranteed a client base through the criminalisation of this association and public money is allocated to the organisations under the pretext that any use of a drug other than alcohol, tobacco and caffeine constitutes a problem requiring a healthcare intervention. Both private and community organisations are allocated public money in order to impose interventions on clients coerced by the criminal justice system.

DRUG TESTING

The testing and detection of substances for employment-related and enforcement purposes has evolved into a lucrative industry. For example, waste water is being monitored for the presence of illicit substances in some countries for no purpose other than to provide economic enterprise funded by public money. Workplace testing of employees to ensure compliance with government regulations in relation to alcohol and illicit drugs is a significant industry in the U.S. and is supported by laws targeting *"businesses interested in doing business with the federal government."* (6 p.16)

The User Accountability program requires that such businesses *"maintain a drug-free workplace principally through educating employees on the dangers of drug abuse, and by informing employees of the penalties they face if they engage in illegal drug activity on company property."* (6 p.16) In order for these companies to secure and maintain work supplying the federal government they may see fit to engage the services of specialist workplace drug-testing companies to assist them in complying with the legislative requirements of the government in respect of being 'drug free'.

The criminalisation of associations with drugs other than alcohol, tobacco and caffeine provides much of the basis for industries such as those providing workplace drug-testing services. The existence of these industries is therefore to a large degree based upon the inequitable treatment of people and relies upon the maintenance of the laws that create the inequity. A system of economic activity that is based upon selective criminalisation and the resultant oppression is therefore created and sustained by a reliable funding source: public money distributed by governments.

ORGANISATIONS THAT SUPPLY GOODS AND SERVICES TO THOSE INVOLVED IN THE GESICC

The resources required to enable the functioning of the Drug Enforcement Administration and the prison industry, for example, are considerable. The businesses that supply them with goods and services are numerous and diverse. From weapons and other military-inspired equipment to asset construction and information technology, the opportunities for business are significant and lucrative and form a dependable source of income.

(This list is by no means conclusive)

WHY AND HOW IT CONTINUES

The policy regime that fundamentally is a human-rights abuse continues unabated imposing cruelty upon a minority on a worldwide scale for the purpose of enabling financial and political gain. Following are some fundamental reasons why a global atrocity persists.

The policy is politically advantageous on two main fronts. Firstly, it allows politicians to give the impression that they are protecting their constituents from an enemy constituting a threat to health and welfare. However, the enemy is contrived and the war to fight it has different motives altogether.

Secondly, governments are able to dispense public money and create jobs and profits using the contrived problem as the justification. The allocation of money is deceptively justified as being necessary to fight and control the supposed enemy and the strategy therefore largely escapes being correctly identified as a form of welfare and blatant largess.

Notably, those employed in law enforcement and those who support them benefit from tens of billions of dollars of public money annually in the U.S. alone. A constant supply-reduction campaign along with demand that will never cease ensures the price of illicit substances remains high. This guarantees the continuance of the trade and results in a self-sustaining and perpetual false war that employs and sustains thousands of people.

Those involved in the black market in illicit drugs benefit from a multi-billion dollar trade. Money from the black market finds its way to the legitimate economy and benefits those involved in regular financial endeavours and, particularly, those who assisted its transition to becoming legitimate money. Under a legal and regulated market, black marketeers would lose their market monopoly and, consequently, their income would be dramatically reduced.

INDUSTRIAL COMPLEX

The GESICC continues primarily because it is financially beneficial to many people. It has direct parallels with the so-called 'military industrial complex' where war or the threat of war provides apparent justifaction for substantial government expenditure. This results in a situation in which many people and industries become reliant upon the funding and, consequently, it is difficult to cease or scale back the process due to loss of income and unemployment being politically unpalatable.

Accordingly, industrial systems and, therefore, economies that are founded on less than favourable circumstances become ingrained and essentially perpetual.

Three industries associated with the GESICC that are easily identified are the enforcement, prison and 'treatment' industries. All three utilise and profit from a human resource that is defined solely by associations with drugs other than alcohol, tobacco and caffeine. No person possessing, using or involved in the lawful supply of alcohol, tobacco, and caffeine is mandated because of these associations as being subject to the activities of these industries.

The enforcement sector consists of police and organisations such as the Drug Enforcement Administration in the United States. The detention of hundreds of thousands of people by the prison industry is funded by public money and involves to some extent private and, therefore, profit-making companies.

The 'treatment' industry is the recipient of substantial amounts of public money and is portrayed as existing to assist people on the basis that they are suffering from a mental disorder due simply to their use of psychoactive substances other than alcohol, tobacco and caffeine.

There are many other examples of entities that rely upon the GESICC for part or all of their income. Once a human-rights abuse becomes the basis for industry, a dangerous cycle of financial and political dependency results that leads to the policy regime and the oppression upon which it is based becoming an enduring phenomenon.

THE PERFECT BUSINESS MODEL

The mechanism that underpins the GESICC could be described as the perfect business model. In relation to enforcement agencies, their activities ensure the existence and vibrancy of the black market by reducing but not eliminating supply. When the supply of a commodity for which there is constant demand is reduced, the price increases. The higher the market price the greater the incentive for people to supply the commodity especially in light of a zero-tax environment.

Consequently, a guaranteed economy of illicit drug supply is created and along with it a perpetual supply of substances to intercept and people to arrest and process. By reducing supply and, thereby, maintaining the vibrancy of the black market, enforcement agencies are simply ensuring the existence of work for themselves. This simple economic cause and effect scenario provides the perfect self-perpetuating economic model.

If the substances were supplied by a legal and regulated market, agencies involved solely in drug-supply reduction activities would have no basis upon which to justify their existence.

In a document listing important organisational statistics, and under the heading "*Revenue Denied*", it is stated that between 2005 and 2014 the Drug Enforcement Administration "*stripped drug trafficking organizations of approximately \$29.6 billion in revenues through the seizure of both assets and drugs*." (13) Asset forfeiture laws enable governments to remove financial gains from those who have been apprehended and gain revenue by forcibly taking money and assets. Asset seizure provides governments with the opportunity to profit from the crime that they have intentionally created and offset a small proportion of the public money allocated to these activities.

Interdiction (intercepting illicit drugs and arresting those distributing and selling them) achieves several important objectives relating to the success and ongoing viability of the GESICC:

• It falsely portrays substances other than alcohol, tobacco and caffeine as comprising a unique threat to the populace due to the existence of a government led supply reduction strategy with the stated aim of protecting people's health and welfare. Because the strategy is government inspired, the illusion of a valid justification for the activity is created.

• It provides the basis for thousands of jobs and a substantial amount of related economic activity including civilian industries engaged in supporting enforcement agencies.

• Interception of illicit substances is publicised widely giving the illusion that the 'war' is being successful and that there are tangible results for the substantial amount of public money expended. In actual fact, only a fraction of the total supply of illicit drugs is intercepted.

• Above all else, it perpetuates the trade in illicit substances by keeping their market price high due to supply reduction. The continuance of the activity is essential for the people and organisations that are funded by public money in order to respond to it.

Enforcement relating to illicit drug supply has evolved into a substantial worldwide industry which is sustained by large amounts of public money. Agencies such as the Drug Enforcement Administration have been created and the funding of other entities involved in enforcement activities has been supplemented based upon this activity.

CRITICAL POINT: *The policy that is represented as a war on drugs is not a failure. It was never intended to control psychoactive substances of any kind as a response to harm resulting from their use. Its aim is the attainment of political advantage which is gained via the distribution of substantial amounts of public money and the maintenance of a highly lucrative black market in drugs other than alcohol, tobacco and caffeine. It is, and has been, an outstanding success in relation to its true motives. This is why it continues. Those who profit from and are sustained by the public money distributed or the black market in illicit substances have no desire for its ending irrespective of the fact that it is based upon the inequitable treatment of a minority.*

ECONOMIC UTILISATION OF A MINORITY

The obvious example of how a minority can be oppressed and exploited purely to facilitate political advantage through financial gain is opioid users. No other subset of people are systematically and aggressively exploited to the degree that those who choose to use opioids are. There is an international industry involved in the production, distribution and sale of illicit opioids and at every level of the system, from production to use, people are liable to sanction from the criminal justice system. People who choose to supply or use opioids are ruthlessly exploited in many and varied ways in order to enable financial gain and political advantage.

Fundamentally, users of opioids are defined by their association with a substance other than alcohol, tobacco and caffeine as being subject to criminalisation. First and foremost, they are denied a legal and regulated supply of their drug of choice which obligates them to obtain it from and, thereby, sustain a black market that comprises a vast worldwide economic system.

Due to being criminalised, they can be subject to involvement in the criminal justice system. As part of this involvement, they can be convicted of a crime. This can be as basic as being in possession of their drug of choice. Being convicted of a crime can result in incarceration. These two circumstances, together or separately, can result in gainful employment being difficult or essentially impossible to attain because of the existence of a criminal record.

This can in turn result in the person being forced to lead a chaotic lifestyle due to being financially impoverished. This situation often results in them resorting to crime in order to survive as usual avenues of obtaining income are unavailable due to the consequences of being criminalised.

Being involved in illegal activities as a means to survival can lead to a self-perpetuating cycle of crime, conviction, incarceration and re-offending. This cycle of crime serves well those entities engaged in the criminal justice and welfare sectors and, therefore, sustained to some degree by public money: enforcement agencies, the legal system, the prison industry, welfare and advocacy organisations and those who supply and support them.

A certain amount of choice is denied to those physically dependent on opioids that is not denied to those dependent on alcohol, tobacco, and caffeine. To prevent experiencing physical withdrawal, opioid users are obliged to commit an offence: possession of an illicit substance. In contrast, users of alcohol, tobacco, and caffeine are able to obtain a legal and regulated supply of their drug of choice in order to prevent experiencing physical withdrawal.

This situation provides the basis for the opioid substitution system. It is based upon the pretext of 'treating' people who use opioids on a consistent basis and it reduces the person's exposure to the black market by supplying an opioid-agonist drug whose manufacture is regulated. Non-medical opioid use is perpetually and aggressively portrayed as being a mental disorder requiring treatment. The specific term in use in the United States is 'Opioid Use Disorder'. The use of opioids on a recreational basis is denied legitimacy and legality and instead framed as a wholly negative phenomenon: a mental disorder that must be treated.

Of course, using an opioid for its effects on the central nervous system is fundamentally the same on a psychological basis as using alcohol for the same purpose. The immediately apparent difference between use of the two substances is that opioids cause constipation whereas alcohol does not. Alcohol is by far the most dangerous drug of the two.

Recreational opioid use is represented as a mental disorder requiring treatment thereby providing the apparent basis for an entire system devoted to 'treating' those who use the substances. Ironically though, so-called 'substitution therapy' is actually the supply of an opioid although it is typically and intentionally not the fundamental opioid sought by users which is morphine.

Methadone is the traditional opioid given as part of opioid substitution therapy. It is a long-acting opioid that is actually more difficult to cease using than morphine. Buprenorphine is an opioid also utilised as part of the so-called 'therapy'. Opioid substitution therapy is ostensibly based upon the assertion that use of the substitute drug is less harmful than the use of heroin. This is wholly incorrect, however, as the primary active metabolite of heroin (morphine) is the prototypical opioid that is used widely in medicine primarily for pain relief and is safe apart from constipation.

The second implication is that the intervention allows the person to lead a less chaotic lifestyle due to the provision of a legal and regulated supply. This is highly deceptive, however, as a chaotic lifestyle was originally and intentionally imposed upon the person by government by way of the denial of a legal and regulated supply of the person's drug of choice thereby deliberately and ironically providing the basis for the intervention.

Framing opioid use as a mental disorder requiring treatment aids the psychological oppression of people by portraying them as mentally unwell simply due to them using a psychoactive substance: the same activity the majority in society engages in on a daily basis and is taken to be a basic right and expectation.

Who benefits from opioid substitution therapy? The predominant beneficiaries are doctors who prescribe and monitor the 'therapy' (often on a long-term basis), pharmaceutical companies that supply the substitute opioid and pharmacies that dispense it. However, the 'treatment' is only available to a limited number of people and it intentionally does not utilise morphine which is the fundamental opioid sought by users.

Consequently, those who desire opioids and cannot find a place in opioid substitution programs or are unable to obtain prescription heroin maintenance are obliged to obtain an illegal and unregulated supply of their drug of choice from the black market. This situation protects the viability and vitality of the black market in heroin and other opioids which is a situation of primary importance to those profiting from the GESICC.

Accordingly, two significant circumstances are achieved. Firstly, the maintenance of a highly lucrative worldwide black market in heroin and other opioids. Secondly, the provision of a system of opioid supply that is deceptively portrayed as being an altruistic and medically justified health intervention. This facilitates the distribution of substantial amounts of public money and, thereby, provides profits for private businesses in addition to generating and maintaining employment in government-funded healthcare services. All these factors provide political advantage.

It is important to recognise that the enabling foundation for both opioid substitution therapy and heroin maintenance programs is the criminalisation of supply and possession of heroin and other opioids. If associations with heroin and other associated substances were not criminalised and people could simply obtain a legal and regulated supply of their drug of choice as the users of alcohol, tobacco, and caffeine are able to do, the opioid substitution system would have no basis upon which to justify its existence.

———————

To provide some context for the opioid substitution system, a hypothetical situation in relation to a similar strategy as applied to use of the most dangerous drug in existence is as follows. The supply and possession of tobacco is criminalised on the basis of protecting health and welfare. Smokers are liable to being apprehended by police for being in possession of and using the substance. Those apprehended are given the choice of a fine or treatment for their drug use. Those who choose treatment are mandated to use nicotine replacement therapy. They are required to attend a pharmacy once a day to obtain a supply of the treatment.

If they, at any time, forgo the treatment and return to acquiring tobacco from the black market, they are liable to being apprehended by police and processed as drug addicts. They are then subject to fines or the alternative intervention of treatment.

This example illustrates the double standard inherent in the application of interventions such as substitution therapy under what is represented as a war on drugs. This intervention would not be enforced upon the users of tobacco simply because, as a generalisation, twenty percent of the population use the drug including politicians and those who work in the enforcement, legal, welfare and treatment industries. This example further illustrates that the GESICC is solely an economic system based upon selective criminalisation and is not concerned with the harm arising from the use of drugs of any kind.

Due to the supply of their drug of choice being criminalised, opioid users are forced to travel to a place where the black market supply is known to be reliable. As many who make the journey to such areas are undergoing or beginning to undergo physical withdrawal, they are eager to administer the drug once they procure it.

Those who have a combination of central nervous system depressant drugs in their body are susceptible to an adverse event related to breathing. As described earlier in this book, this is when a combination of depressant drugs causes profound and disabling sedation that can lead to the person being unable to control their airway. This makes them vulnerable to airway obstruction and the possibility of asphyxiation.

This chain of events can result in regular ambulance attendances to treat the afflicted. This can lead to resident unrest and prompt the establishment of so-called 'medically supervised injecting centres'. These facilities are staffed by medically trained personnel who can assist in the event of someone suffering problematic sedation due to the ingestion of multiple depressant substances and, consequently, being in danger of airway obstruction.

The facilities can assist those suffering problematic sedation by the provision of airway support and the possible administration of naloxone which removes the opioid-induced component of the sedation. The facilities are rich sources of funding for those in the health and welfare sectors and are enthusiastically advocated for by those who seek to benefit from the money and subsequent employment opportunities provided.

However, the fundamental issue is that opioid users have a chaotic lifestyle enforced upon them and must travel to areas in which the black market supply of opioids is known to be reliable. If supply and possession of their drug of choice was not subject to criminalisation they would procure it close to their places of residence and administer the substance at a time and place convenient to them. Their lifestyles would therefore be the same in this respect as those for whom the supply and possession of their drug of choice is legal.

They would be less likely to combine substances due to having a reliable and legal supply of opioids and, therefore, less vulnerable to adverse events related to mixed-drug toxicity Honest acknowledgement and education about the hazards of combining depressant drugs would allow people the opportunity to use safely.

Medically supervised injecting centres are universally and deceptively portrayed by governments and others advocating for their existence as providing a service that saves users from the consequences of an overdose of opioids. This falsehood is used as the primary basis and justification for the establishment and promotion of the facilities. There is never any public acknowledgement by those operating the centres that the interventions provided are related to sedation caused by the ingestion of multiple classes of depressant drugs. There is generally an unwavering and universal failure to clearly communicate the truth in relation to this matter.

The deceptive and incorrect implication conveyed by governments that medically supervised injecting centres are required for the safe use of opioids due to the danger presented by overdose allows them to further reinforce the falsehood of supply and use of opioids being criminalised in order to protect health and welfare. This, in turn, provides the opportunity for governments to further justify existing policy that includes the criminalisation of users and the existence and vibrancy of the worldwide black market in opioids.

Establishment of the facilities allows governments to foster political advantage by distributing considerable sums of public money. This facilitates increased employment and provides financial security for non-governmental organisations engaged in the health and welfare sector and those who supply and support them.

Governments represent themselves as acting in a compassionate manner towards opioid users by providing the centres when in reality they are engaged in aggressive and systematic oppression of the people who use them by criminalising the supply and possession of their drug of choice.

The organisations promoting interventions such as medically supervised injecting centres never publicly acknowledge that an overdose of heroin does not cause dangerous compromise of breathing and that the salient issue is combinations of central nervous system depressant drugs initiated intentionally or unintentionally by the user. Nor do they acknowledge that underpinning the difficulties of users of drugs other than alcohol, tobacco and caffeine is selective criminalisation and subsequent economic exploitation.

As a generalisation, they concentrate only on advocating for interventions that provide funding and profits with little or no concern for the nature of the rationale utilised. Unfortunately, the welfare sector benefits to a degree from the selective criminalisation of people utilised by the GESICC: people who in many instances become their clients as a direct result of the difficulties created by the criminalisation.

Naloxone is a competitive opioid antagonist which means it displaces opioids from their receptors in the central nervous system but does not exert an effect. When people are affected by profound sedation caused by a combination of central nervous system depressant drugs including opioids it can remove the opioid-induced component of the sedation and allow the person to regain consciousness. However, the drug is being aggressively marketed as the primary intervention in the recreational setting on the incorrect basis that people are succumbing solely to overdoses of opioid drugs.

Profound sedation from a combination of central nervous system depressant drugs renders an individual incapable of administering the substance themselves so if the person is affected whilst alone naloxone is of no benefit. Disturbingly but unsurprisingly, the drug is being promoted heavily by some welfare and advocacy groups in the absence of an accurate narrative about the effects of combining depressant drugs and that the critical intervention is airway protection. The failure by some organisations to be open and honest about the issue of mixed-drug toxicity is ultimately an indication of their degree of actual concern for the welfare of, especially, those who use alone.

In summary, the criminalisation of supply and possession of a drug of choice, in this case opioids, provides many lucrative funding opportunities for a variety of organisations and the people employed by them. The pharmaceutical industry, the governmental and non-governmental welfare and healthcare sectors, academia and those who supply and support them are amongst those who can benefit financially from the criminalisation and economic utilisation of a minority. This income is welcomed by these sectors with apparently little concern for the oppression and suffering upon which the distribution of money is based.

THE BENEFITS OF BEING LEGAL

Current 'drug policy' suits the alcohol, tobacco and caffeine industries admirably. They (particularly in the case of alcohol and caffeine) are able to benefit from essentially unrestricted advertising and marketing of their products. They are able to freely link their products with sport and other types of entertainment and gain widespread media coverage with little in the way of regulation.

The greatest advantage for the legal drug industry is that supply and use of alternative drugs and, therefore, the commercial competition is subject to criminal sanctions. They are also served well by the false portrayal of drugs that are an alternative to alcohol, tobacco and caffeine as uniquely dangerous and socially unacceptable. It is the perfect commercial situation for the alcohol, tobacco and caffeine industries.

It could be suggested that their greatest fear is drugs other than alcohol, tobacco and caffeine becoming legal and freely available. Market share of the three currently legal drugs (alcohol, tobacco and caffeine) would be threatened by increased commercial competition. A genuine and equitable system of regulation that treated substances according to their actual danger would also be a less than ideal situation for the alcohol and tobacco industries in particular.

The 'debate' about whether drugs other than alcohol, tobacco and caffeine should be legalised is a misleading and dishonest conversation. The more relevant suggestion is that since current 'drug policy' is allegedly about protecting health and welfare it follows that supply and possession of alcohol, tobacco and caffeine should also be criminalised. This simple and obvious suggestion instantly exposes the fraudulent nature of the policy regime.

POLITICIANS

The silence from politicians regarding the true nature of the policy they portray as addressing harm resulting from drug use is complete and resolute on a worldwide basis. Interestingly, the silence extends to those parties representing themselves as enthusiastic champions of human rights. I have never witnessed a politician vary from the false narrative that the policy is in place to protect health and welfare. There is a worthwhile discussion to be had examining the reasons for this.

The strategy delivers political advantage due to politicians successfully representing themselves as protecting the populace from a threat to health and welfare. This ploy has been proven to be extremely effective as a method of courting and securing votes on an agenda of community safety. They are obviously reluctant to relinquish this advantage.

The portrayal of politicians as protecting the populace from a threat to health and welfare provides the pretext under which large sums of public money are distributed thereby enabling the creation of economic activity manifesting as jobs and profits. The distribution of public money is an extremely effective way of creating political advantage.

Politicians are obviously fearful of the ramifications if they were to defy the United States on any aspect of the GESICC. Politicians are not in the habit of defying the wishes of a global superpower. The U.S. has ruthlessly maintained the regime over a considerable period of time and has the ability to gain essentially complete compliance using the power inherent in relationships involving military alliances and trade, for example.

Politicians have remained resolute for over fifty years about the nature of 'drug policy'. It is deceptively portrayed as an intervention to protect the populace from harm to health and welfare due to the use of psychoactive substances. From the perspective of politicians wishing to be perceived by the voting public as honest and genuine, an admission by a politician and their administration that 'drug policy' is a blatant deception will never occur.

The worldwide black market in drugs other than alcohol, tobacco and caffeine plays a highly significant role in the global economy so, accordingly, its loss would be a source of concern for politicians and others. Its ability to generate unofficial cash income on the scale of hundreds of billions of dollars annually apparently makes it a phenomenon to be protected and perpetuated by politicians and their administrations regardless of the fact that it is based upon a human-rights abuse.

Unfortunately, there are many reasons why politicians as a whole will continue to support a system of intentionally-created crime and, thereby, perpetuate the oppression of a minority in society for the purpose of enabling economic and political gain. There are a host of factors that lead to politicians universally refusing to acknowledge the true nature of the policy that is represented as being protective of health and welfare in relation to the use of psychoactive substances.

Self-interest and fear make a potent combination in relation to them actively participating in perpetuating a human-rights atrocity whilst in power or in opposition. Ultimately, politicians are either fully supportive of the so-called 'War on Drugs' continuing or not prepared to be involved in the politically challenging activity of confronting the deception that most have utilised for decades to assist them in being elected. The complicit silence on the part of politicians has been resolute for fifty years including those portraying themselves as staunch upholders of human rights.

THE MEDIA

The media plays a crucial role in perpetuating the GESICC. Fundamentally, this involves the constant reinforcement of the falsehood that the strategy is in place to protect health and welfare in relation to the use of psychoactive substances. Drugs other than alcohol, tobacco and caffeine are constantly demonised and portrayed as the predominant threat to health and welfare in relation to substance use while alcohol and caffeine are advertised and promoted at every opportunity.

Myths and misrepresentations are employed to assist in perpetuating the GESICC and the truth about the strategy is meticulously prevented from being disseminated. For example, in the event of a television panel discussion occurring on the subject, the participants are selected so as to guarantee the content presented does not contain discussion that may give any insight into the actual nature of the policy. Former law-enforcement personnel and those funded by public money are commonly enlisted to present the required narrative.

One strategy utilised on a frequent basis is describing a death in which drugs have been present as a 'drug overdose' before any proper investigation has been undertaken. In situations in which a parent has embarked upon a career of awareness raising after having lost a child to multiple-drug toxicity involving opioids, the incident is consistently, mischievously and incorrectly reported decades later as being a heroin overdose.

The media often aggressively portrays people who use drugs other than alcohol, tobacco and caffeine as deviant and deserving of any misfortune that may befall them. Associations with illicit substances are often utilised in order to demonise and, thereby, incorrectly portray users of illicit substances as being inherently troublesome members of society.

The media in all its forms is utilised for the purposes of propagandising and reinforcing myths, prejudices and misconceptions. Its ability to profoundly influence the beliefs of the populace proves invaluable in perpetuating the fear that is the basis of the policy regime. The public narrative is controlled and maintained in order to achieve the continuance of a worldwide economic system based upon intentionally-created crime with the widespread support of the public.

A COMPLICIT SILENCE

From those in receipt of public money distributed on the basis of the GESICC, there is a resolute and uniform worldwide silence regarding the strategy's actual intentions and consequences. The dominant narrative is that 'drug policy' is a failure and needs to be modified so as not to have such a devastating impact on those affected by it. This narrative is based upon the falsehood that the underlying goal of the policy is the prevention and minimisation of harm due to the use of drugs. Not under any circumstances will anyone benefiting from the policy admit that it has as its foundation the distribution of public money facilitated by the criminalisation and subsequent economic utilisation of a minority.

This situation exists simply because no matter what those who benefit from the GESICC think about its exploitative and abusive mechanisms, they are willing to remain silent as long as it puts money in their pockets and food on the table There are many for whom receipt of some or all of their funding is based upon responding to factors that are largely or entirely caused by the selective criminalisation and subsequent economic utilisation of people that underpins the GESICC.

There exists a worldwide network of welfare and advocacy organisations that are ostensibly working to bring about change on the basis that the policy is inequitable and cruel to people. Many of these bodies publicly represent themselves as being passionate about ending the 'War on Drugs' and as fighting to end or ameliorate the oppression associated with it. However, many of these organisations are funded by public money distributed by governments: administrations that are committed to perpetuating the economic and political gain facilitated by the GESICC.

Without exception, these organisations remain resolutely loyal to their funding sources and will not under any circumstances deviate from the false and deceptive narrative that the policy is in place to protect people from harm due to the use of psychoactive substances. They have a grim and flippant solidarity in asserting that the policy regime needs modification of its structure and application rather than acknowledge that it is solely a system based upon the economic exploitation of a minority enabled by selective criminalisation and, therefore, by its very nature, oppression.

Invariably, they call for more money to be devoted to harm reduction which is one of the three pillars of the strategy designated as harm minimisation and based upon the falsehood of 'drug policy' being in place to protect health and welfare. Demand reduction, supply reduction and harm reduction are the three components that supposedly underpin international governmental response to harm caused by the use of psychoactive substances both licit and illicit. However, the strategy does not stand up to the most basic scrutiny: there is no supply reduction or mandated 'treatment', for example, in relation to alcohol, tobacco and caffeine use.

The harm is portrayed as resulting from the use of illicit drugs but the vast majority of the harm experienced is actually caused by the criminalisation and subsequent economic exploitation imposed by the GESICC. Money allocated under the banner of harm minimisation forms part or all of the income for many organisations who have client bases comprised of those whose lives are made chaotic due to the imposition of criminalisation upon them as part of the GESICC.

Public money distributed has with it an inherent and effective quid pro quo: that the recipients of the funding do not give any public indication that the basis of 'drug policy' is intentionally-created crime facilitated by the criminalisation of a minority. Any such admission by the organisations would immediately endanger their funding and, therefore, their viability. Accordingly, they remain silent about the atrocity that assists in sustaining them.

The silence in regard to the actual nature of the 'War on Drugs' by those who represent themselves as fighting to end the phenomenon is a salient reminder of the political power that accompanies the distribution of public money. Those in receipt of the money have an unshakeable loyalty to the providers of the funding that includes turning a blind eye to the human-rights abuse and cynical political strategy that forms the very basis for distribution of the money.

The silence extends beyond those organisations portrayed as existing for the purposes of welfare and advocacy. Organisations representing themselves as specialising in human rights are also silent in relation to the true nature of what is represented as a war on drugs. A worldwide human-rights abuse involving mass incarceration, capital punishment and endemic violence is apparently not deserving of a genuine conversation involving organisations representing themselves as having the sole purpose of working towards the cessation of situations that involve oppression and suffering.

DECEPTIVE TERMS AND CONCEPTS

There are four notable and persistent falsehoods regarding the GESICC offered by those who benefit from it and, accordingly, wish for it to continue. The first one is that the so-called 'War on Drugs' has failed. This theme is by far the most dominant narrative, is omnipresent on social media and consistently emanates from those in receipt of public money.

The rationale for describing it as a failure is that it is intended as a strategy to prevent and minimise the availability and use of psychoactive substances on the grounds of protecting health and welfare and, consequently, the availability and use of drugs has not been prevented or minimised. But of course, this rationale is obviously both incorrect and deceptive.

The strategy was never intended to prevent and minimise the use of drugs on the basis of protecting health and welfare as evidenced by the fact that associations with alcohol, tobacco and caffeine are not addressed. In relation to any harm caused by illicit drugs, the strategy can only maximise this due to the unregulated manufacture of substances, for example.

The GESICC intentionally creates a lucrative worldwide black market in drugs other than alcohol, tobacco and caffeine by criminalising supply of the substances. The policy intentionally and very efficiently creates the perfect environment for maximum production and distribution of illicit drugs through the incentive of large, tax-free profits. This situation ensures the enthusiastic involvement of people in the enterprise. The strategy was never intended to minimise the supply and use of drugs other than alcohol, tobacco and caffeine.

The assertion that a political strategy that has been in progress in a highly organised and ruthlessly enforced form for half a century is a failure is one that can only be described as deceptive or naive. A political strategy that results in large amounts of public money being distributed and the existence and maintenance of a lucrative worldwide black market in illicit drugs can only credibly be described as wholly intentional and extremely successful.

Politicians and their parties are not in the habit of perpetuating policy deemed failed for decade after decade. To do so would not be conducive to political survival. If a policy is at any time in its history recognised as truly being a failure it is terminated immediately so as not to be a political liability.

Politicians are certainly not in the habit of wasting large sums of public money repeatedly. Public money is seldom subject to a distribution process that results in waste: there is always a politically calculated rationale behind the allocation of funds derived from taxpayers. A substantial amount of scrutiny regarding who is receiving the money and the resultant political advantage takes place well in advance of its distribution.

The amount of money devoted to the strategy in the United States alone has been on the scale of hundreds of billions of dollars over a period of half a century. Obviously, for there to be expenditure on this scale and persisting for this period of time, the policy is wholly politically advantageous and, accordingly, overwhelmingly successful in relation to its true motives.

Portrayal of the policy as failed is suppression of the fact that it is an aggressive strategy of economic exploitation and not concerned in any way with the prevention or minimisation of drug-related harm. Describing it as failed policy allows those who benefit from it to represent themselves as being concerned about its impact on people when they are presumably content for it to continue due to being sustained by the money distributed under it.

A commonly encountered deceptive term emanating from those unwilling to give an honest and basic account of the GESICC is 'drug policy'. It is often deceptively or naively described as failed or based upon good intentions but ultimately flawed, for example.

The implication is that so-called 'drug policy' is an overarching and genuine response by government to drug-related harm. This is, of course, patent nonsense. What is represented as drug policy is based upon the Controlled Substances Act and its equivalents and does not address associations with the two most dangerous drugs in existence (alcohol and tobacco) and caffeine.

Drug policy, as it is referred to, is not policy about drugs and drug-related harm: it is policy that facilitates oppressive economic utilisation of a minority by way of selective criminalisation. Policy genuinely concerned with drug-related harm cannot exclude associations with alcohol, tobacco and caffeine. True drug policy would include a response to the supply, possession and use of alcohol, tobacco and caffeine utilising the same mechanisms applied to other drugs.

Another deceptive assertion commonly encountered is that policy which deems the supply and possession of drugs other than alcohol, tobacco and caffeine as an offence is a response to the condition known as 'addiction'. The term is commonly used to describe compulsive use with or without the existence of problematic consequences. The common implication is that 'addiction' is a condition having wholly negative consequences and only applies to those who use drugs other than alcohol, tobacco and caffeine.

Those who use the term 'addiction' commonly apply the word when the substance involved in a circumstance that is portrayed as being inherently harmful in nature is opioids: morphine and its equivalents. However, discourse using the term consistently in reference to the use of opioids inherently contains multiple concepts that fall short of being honest and correct. Firstly, the assertion that compulsive and regular use of a drug is only encountered in those using opioids, for example, is obviously incorrect. A sizeable proportion of the world's population is physically dependent on caffeine. As a generalisation, twenty per cent of the world's population is physically dependent on tobacco which is the most dangerous drug in existence. If what is represented as drug policy was actually a response to 'addiction' it would apply in the first instance to the users of caffeine.

Secondly, the assertion that the use of opioids arbitrarily comes with a set of negative consequences is completely untrue and mischievous. Opioid users who have chaotic lifestyles caused by financial and/or legal circumstances relating to possession of the substances are simply victims of selective criminalisation imposed upon them by governments. Their troubles are almost entirely the result of the criminalisation of supply and possession of their drug of choice which is a situation intentionally enforced upon them to enable political advantage via the distribution of public money and the existence of a worldwide black market in recreational opioids.

Furthermore, given a legal and regulated supply of opioids, the primary troublesome consequence of use is constipation. Tobacco use is associated with a host of cancers, respiratory diseases and cardio-vascular disorders. Opioid use is associated with nausea and constipation. To imply that the policy represented as a war on drugs is largely a response to opioid use would be to assert that the U.S. spends billions of dollars annually implementing measures such as arrest, imprisonment and asset seizure to prevent and minimise constipation in a tiny minority of its citizens. Obviously, this is not the case and never will be the case.

Finally, the term 'overdose'. The term is used persistently and aggressively to incorrectly portray illicit substances as possessing a unique capability of causing injury or death due to the simple act of taking 'too much'. For example, the persistent assertion is that an overdose of heroin can result in dangerous compromise or cessation of breathing and, consequently, injury or death. As has been described in detail in this book, there is no evidence to support this assertion and the evidence that does exist proves the concept is a fallacy.

It is wholly implausible that governments are not well aware that overdose of heroin does not cause injury or death and that the danger is profound sedation from combinations of central nervous system depressant drugs leading to breathing problems. However, this does not stop the media, in particular, from immediately attributing a death in which opioids or other illicit drugs are present to a process they describe as 'overdose' and, therefore, by implication that the event was caused solely by an excessive amount of an illicit substance.

Governments are determined to incorrectly portray opioid use, in particular, as uniquely dangerous and, therefore, apparently deserving of oppressive measures to control supply and use of the drug on the grounds of protecting health and welfare. The result of the strategy is, however, completely avoidable injury and death as many users incorrectly believe that the danger associated with opioid use is overdose and, therefore, are not mindful of the actual hazard which is combinations of depressant drugs.

The blatant semantic deception arising from use of the term 'overdose' is universally and effectively utilised by governments, the media and others. The term is used in an all-encompassing manner effectively preventing public awareness of multiple-drug toxicity and its contribution to adverse events. Use of the term 'overdose' to describe a situation arising from the combining of substances is deceptive and blatantly irresponsible. A failure to be open and honest about multiple-drug toxicity is simply to have a degree of culpability in any deaths arising from the phenomenon.

The term is the standard catchcry for the media regardless of the circumstances surrounding the event. Disturbingly, the refrain has been augmented and use of the term 'suspected overdose' has become commonplace as a method of creating alarm and instilling fear on the basis of a complete lack of evidence. The use of this term very effectively confirms the intention of those who use it as instilling fear in the mind of the public in relation to drugs other than alcohol, tobacco and caffeine with a ruthless and arrogant enthusiasm.

The use of deceptive and misleading language is a common occurrence when illicit substances are involved and is a tool used to create fear, reinforce incorrect stereotypes and, ultimately, to assist in perpetuating the GESICC.

DECRIMINALISATION

The approach of Portugal regarding the criminalisation of people as defined by their associations with drugs other than alcohol, tobacco and caffeine is popularly held up as an alternative to the situation that exists worldwide. It is asserted by some that the possession of illicit drugs has been 'decriminalised' in the country and that the approach taken is therefore fundamentally different to the norm and a sign of progressive policy change.

The possession of such drugs has been 'decriminalised' only in terms of the offence being classified under certain circumstances as administrative rather than criminal in nature. Possession of drugs other than alcohol, tobacco and caffeine remains an offence and one for which people continue to be processed by authorities. If a person is apprehended in possession of controlled substances, the drugs are confiscated by police. If the person is unable to be identified at the time of apprehension, they can be detained.

A person can be dealt with in an administrative manner for possession of controlled substances when the drugs found are deemed as being for the person's own consumption and the amount does not exceed that required for average consumption by an individual over a period of ten days. People found in possession of amounts for personal use are processed by the so-called 'Commission for the Dissuasion of Drug Addiction'.

Substances that are controlled in the country and, therefore, carry criminal and administrative sanctions for associations with them are defined in tables I to IV of Decree-Law No. 15/93 of 22 January. Alcohol, tobacco and caffeine are not controlled substances and, therefore, the suppliers and users of these three drugs are not subject to criminal or administrative sanctions when engaged in possession, use, and lawful supply activities.

The situation in Portugal does not represent any actual change to the policy of intentionally creating crime for the purpose of enabling financial and political gain by using an association with particular substances to define those criminalised. An association with a controlled drug without official justification such as a medical prescription remains an offence in the country and continues to be subject to intervention by authorities.

Law No. 30/2000 of 29 November is the law that details the processing of people arrested for possession of psychoactive substances subject to control in Portugal.

In November of 2020 and to great fanfare amongst welfare and advocacy groups in the U.S., Measure 110 or the Drug Addiction Treatment and Recovery Act was passed in Oregon. It was portrayed by proponents as being substantive change to 'drug policy'. However, similar to the approach in Portugal, supply and possession of controlled substances remains unlawful. The supply and possession of methadone, oxycodone, heroin, MDMA, cocaine and methamphetamine remains unlawful and is therefore an offence.

In Oregon, an offence is *"conduct for which a sentence to a term of imprisonment or to a fine is provided by any law of this state"*. (18) An offence can be a crime or a violation. A crime is defined by the ability of the state to impose a prison sentence. Crimes are categorised as misdemeanors or felonies depending on the length of prison sentence able to be imposed.

The sanction for possession of small amounts of the above listed substances was changed from a misdemeanour (which allows for a prison sentence) to a violation carrying a fine of *"$100, or, in lieu of the fine, a completed health assessment"*. (19 p.15) Accordingly, possession of small amounts of controlled substances has been decriminalised only in relation to the offence no longer being technically classified as a crime (which allows for the imposition of a prison sentence). (Refer Add.)

Those found in possession of larger amounts of controlled substances will continue to be committing an offence classified as a misdemeanor (a crime) for which a custodial sentence may be imposed. It is fundamentally incorrect to unconditionally assert that possession of controlled substances has been decriminalised in the state of Oregon. (Refer Add.)

People will continue to be apprehended by police and processed as defined by the substance they associate with via the act of supply or possession when that substance is controlled. They will continue to be guilty of committing an offence. No person possessing, using or engaging in lawful supply of the drugs alcohol, tobacco, caffeine, and cannabis will be apprehended and processed due solely to an association with the particular substance.

The defining characteristic of the law is a significant expansion of the state's 'treatment' sector with dramatic increases in funding courtesy of revenue generated by taxes imposed upon the supply of cannabis. There is reference in the Act to "moneys allocated from the Oregon Marijuana Account". (19 p.6) Tens of millions of dollars is to be allocated to the newly created Drug

97

Treatment and Recovery Services Fund with the stipulation that "*The total amount deposited and transferred into the fund shall not be less than $57 million for the first year this Act is in effect*". (19 p.6)

References are made to the establishment of Addiction Recovery Centers and "*that at least one center shall be established within each existing coordinated care organization service area*". The Oversight and Accountability Council is to "*provide grants to existing agencies or organizations, whether government or community-based*" to enable the establishment and operation of the centres. (19 p.2)

Several references are made in the preamble of the Act proclaiming that it is a response to 'addiction'. The implication is that people are apprehended and processed with a view to treating them for a mental disorder. The simple act of possessing a controlled substance apparently defines the person as suffering from 'addiction' and, therefore, requiring intervention by the state with mechanisms such as imprisonment, fines or referral to 'treatment'.

It is stated in the preamble that "*Oregon needs to shift its focus to addressing drugs through a humane, cost-effective, health approach*" and that "*Oregon still treats addiction as a criminal problem*". (19 p.1) However, the state of Oregon does not address the use of or addiction to the drugs alcohol, tobacco, caffeine, and cannabis by intervening with apprehension by police and sanctions imposed by the state such as imprisonment, fines or 'treatment'. The state does not proclaim the existence of a problem defined as 'addiction' in relation to substances that are not controlled. The fundamental intention is to facilitate the distribution of public money based upon the economic utilisation of a minority: those who are defined by their associations with controlled substances.

The Drug Addiction Treatment and Recovery Act could only be genuine as a response to drug use and the condition of 'addiction' (however it may be defined) if it mandated mechanisms such as fines, imprisonment and referrals to 'treatment' for those found in possession of any psychoactive substance including alcohol, tobacco, caffeine and cannabis.

In summary, the approach of so-called 'decriminalisation' measures is characterised by two main circumstances. Firstly, the retention of an offence for supply and possession of substances deemed controlled in the particular jurisdiction. Secondly, and as a consequence of the previous circumstance, the continuation of the defining and subsequent utilisation of people for economic and political purposes.

The strategy of 'decriminalisation' is used to misrepresent changes in the nature of penalties as being substantive change in relation to the policy of defining people for economic utilisation. The only way true decriminalisation and, therefore, the cessation of the defining of people for economic exploitation can be achieved is by the acts of supply, possession and use of illicit drugs no longer being deemed an offence: in other words, by legalising all psychoactive substances.

MANDATED TREATMENT

Any person who believes their substance use has become problematic has the right to seek assistance from a welfare or healthcare provider that offers an appropriate service. However, when people are mandated by law to undergo 'treatment' solely on the basis of possessing a drug other than alcohol, tobacco and caffeine, the intervention is obviously not in relation to any desire to protect the health and welfare of the person.

There are no mandated interventions such as fines or 'treatment' imposed upon people on the basis of an association with a drug that is not listed in the Controlled Substances Act or the relevant equivalent. There is no desire by governments to force a user of the drugs alcohol, tobacco, caffeine or (as is the case in Oregon) cannabis to submit to a process described as 'treatment'.

Therefore, the mandated intervention referred to as 'treatment' is largely not intended to assist people regarding their health and welfare in relation to substance use: it is simply an industry funded by public money whose purpose is to provide profits and employment. The intervention referred to as 'treatment' is imposed solely upon a minority who is defined by their use of drugs other than alcohol, tobacco and caffeine in order to utilise them for the financial gain of others. This intervention is not imposed upon those who comprise the majority in society in relation to the use of psychoactive substances.

The strategy referred to as 'decriminalisation' has a fundamental relationship with the defining of the human resource that is utilised by the 'treatment' industry. Decriminalisation does not change the fundamental situation of a minority being defined for economic utilisation by the Controlled Substances Act and its equivalents as associations with drugs other than alcohol, tobacco and caffeine remain an offence.

This situation is illustrated by the actions of organisations who are seeking to benefit from the public money distributed under the pretext of 'treatment'. They advocate strongly for 'decriminalisation' but are silent about the continuation of the defining of a minority by law for the purpose of economic exploitation. The strategy of 'decriminalisation' allows for the continued economic utilisation of a minority with the 'treatment' industry taking advantage of the public money allocated by government in order to provide the coerced intervention. In essence, 'decriminalisation' involves the diversion of a proportion of an intentionally-created human resource from the prison industry to an industry providing an intervention described as 'treatment'.

A CERTAIN MALEVOLENCE

The degree of aggression that typifies the GESICC is starkly detailed in the Drug Enforcement Administration's (U.S.) publication 'Drugs of Abuse'. In the document and in reference to the Anti-Drug Abuse Act of 1988, it speaks of *"a provision in the law that makes public housing projects drug-free"* by allowing for the eviction of *"those residents who allow their units to be used for illegal drug activity"*. (6 pp. 16-17)

The law also provides for the denial of *"federal benefits such as housing assistance and student loans, to individuals convicted of illegal drug activity."* It notes that *"Depending on the offense, an individual may be prohibited from ever receiving any benefit provided by the federal government."* (6 p.17)

These measures illustrate an aggressive desire to make the lives of a minority chaotic. Such a lifestyle invites, and makes more likely, involvement in the criminal justice system. These provisions in law amply demonstrate the human capacity for hostility and cruelty and the alarming ease with which a minority is preyed upon and utilised for the gain of others. Perhaps more disturbing is the fact that behaviour of this nature towards fellow human beings is enshrined in law and, consequently, perpetuated.

HUMAN RIGHTS

It is patently obvious that for the GESICC to exist there must also be a complete lack of meaningful and effective mechanisms to protect human rights. There cannot perhaps be a more blatant human-rights abuse than the intentional criminalisation and subsequent economic utilisation of a minority.

There is much discussion and rhetoric emanating from governments and non-governmental organisations purporting to be the watchdogs of and supporters of human rights regarding legislative protection to prevent and deter the exploitation of people. However, the reality is that a blatant and gratuitous human-rights abuse, the so-called 'War on Drugs', has been ravaging the world for half a century and this situation has been duly supported by a complete absence of effective legislative measures to protect people from the inequity, brutality and exploitation upon which it is based.

LIFE AFTER
THE WAR ON DRUGS

There is only one appropriate action to end the current worldwide human-rights abuse. This is the cessation of intentionally-created crime based upon the criminalisation of people as defined by associations with drugs other than alcohol, tobacco and caffeine. The global economic system based upon intentionally-created crime that has the prevention of drug-related harm as its false and deceptive justification must end.

There must be a return to the legal and regulated manufacture and sale of all psychoactive substances with no person being criminalised due to an association with a drug other than alcohol, tobacco and caffeine. All substances must be available to people of legal age at retail outlets specialising in the supply of recreational psychoactive substances.

This might best be achieved in an incremental way: substance by substance. This would allow people to become accustomed to the situation and realise that the functioning of society and the welfare of people would not be negatively affected. To the contrary, a much more equitable and peaceful world would result.

For most people, the usual reaction to the suggestion of what might be called 'legalisation' is an onset of fear. This is due purely to an ingrained perception of threat and the resultant fear that has been instilled by decades of propaganda. People have been very effectively led to believe that the policy known as the 'War on Drugs' is a response to drug-related harm.

However, once it is understood and accepted that the policy regime is not concerned in any way with preventing and minimising drug-related harm, the solution is simple and achievable. Accordingly, three basic steps required to achieve an end to the atrocity are as follows:

• Those whose drug of choice is alcohol, tobacco, and caffeine are not criminalised as defined by an association with the particular substance. The mere suggestion that users of any of these three drugs be criminalised as defined by their substance use would rightfully be dismissed. The scenario would never and should never eventuate. Therefore:

"No person shall be criminalised as defined by an association with a psychoactive substance of any kind."

105

- Currently, the supply of drugs other than alcohol, tobacco and caffeine is criminalised in order to create and maintain a highly profitable black market. Therefore:

> *"All psychoactive substances without exception must be supplied by a legal and regulated market."*

- The current policy regime is in large part a mechanism to enable the distribution of public money in order to create economic activity. Therefore:

> *"The distribution of public money shall not be based upon the criminalisation and subsequent exploitation of any person."*

The basis of the GESICC is the creation of political advantage via two primary mechanisms: the distribution of public money and financial gain from the black market in drugs other than alcohol, tobacco and caffeine. It can only ever result in cruelty and suffering: it can never be equitable, positive or conducive to a civil society.

This is the heart of the matter: the policy represented as a war on drugs is not about preventing and minimising drug-related harm. It is solely an economic system based upon intentionally-created crime. The prevention and minimisation of drug-related harm is merely the false and deceptive justification for the existence of the phenomenon. It has no concern whatsoever for the health and welfare of people in relation to the use of drugs of any kind.

As has been emphasised at the beginning of this book, the suppliers and users of the two most dangerous drugs in existence (alcohol and tobacco) and caffeine are not criminalised in relation to associations with the substances as the policy regime is not concerned with preventing or minimising drug-related harm.

The primary consideration in affecting genuine change in respect to the so-called 'War on Drugs' is the cessation of a worldwide economic system based upon intentionally-created crime and facilitated by the criminalisation of a minority. It is about ceasing a global economic system that is based upon crime and has as its lifeblood public money distributed by governments and money generated by the worldwide black market in drugs other than alcohol, tobacco and caffeine.

The legalisation of associations with drugs other than alcohol, tobacco and caffeine is merely the removal of the mechanism (criminalisation) that enables the economic utilisation of the minority. It would simply involve the legal supply and possession of currently illicit substances as is the situation with alcohol, tobacco and caffeine. It could only result in a more equitable and peaceful world due to the cessation of the intentionally-created crime utilised by the GESICC.

LEGAL AND REGULATED SUPPLY

The common reaction from people when the establishment of a legal and regulated supply of currently illicit substances is discussed is a concern that young people may increase their use of drugs that are perceived as being harmful to them. A response to this concern is as follows.

A concern that the health and welfare of the young would suddenly be put at risk by a legal and regulated supply of currently illicit drugs is based upon the assumption that so-called 'drug policy' has had a protective role regarding the young by deterring use and reducing supply of the drugs. This assumption is patently and unequivocally incorrect.

From the perspective of use by the young of psychoactive substances, there are two distinct and independent issues. Firstly, regarding harm resulting from the use of recreational drugs, the most dangerous drug for the young is alcohol. For those concerned about the health and welfare of the young in relation to substance use, alcohol is the drug of most concern. Alcohol is freely available in most societies.

Secondly, there is already widespread and enthusiastic use of drugs other than alcohol, tobacco and caffeine by the young. Current laws intentionally put in place a vibrant black market in these substances. From the perspective of availability of the drugs, the black market provides the perfect financial incentive for the supply of illicit substances to the young. From the perspective of safety, the manufacture of these substances is unregulated and this presents a situation in which users have no guarantee of the quality or dose of the drugs they purchase. This situation can have negative consequences for their health and welfare.

That currently illicit substances are not regulated in relation to their manufacture and sale is due solely to governments worldwide legislating so as drugs other than alcohol, tobacco and caffeine are supplied by an unregulated black market. It is not related in any way to preventing and minimising use of the substances on the basis of protecting health and welfare. The strategy can only add a degree of uncertainty and risk to their use.

A legal and regulated market for currently illicit substances simply means that the young would have access to a legal and quality assured supply of substances less dangerous than alcohol. A legal and regulated supply of these drugs may or may not result in an increased rate of use of the substances. A contribution to any increase in use, should it happen, would likely be people using the substances in preference to alcohol due to them presenting a lesser risk to health and welfare.

In order to illustrate the salient point in relation to the regulated supply of drugs, no one would propose that alcohol be supplied by the black market (and its manufacture therefore being unregulated) as a way of protecting the health and welfare of the young.

A legal and regulated market simply gives assurance as to the nature and quality of the substance and the concentration of the active ingredient is known to the user. The consumer can have confidence that the product is what it is represented to be and they can subsequently make a decision regarding their use of the substance including any potential consequences for their health and welfare.

Given this situation, those who are concerned about a legal and regulated market for currently illicit drugs are, by definition, not supportive of measures providing for the welfare of those who use the substances. This course of action is not conducive to the welfare of those who use the drugs or to a civil society in general.

So accordingly, from the perspective of the safety of the young in relation to the use of psychoactive substances, it is clear that the current policy regime maximises risks to their health and welfare from a variety of perspectives.

A legal and regulated market for currently illicit drugs would simply involve the existence of two circumstances.

Firstly, young people would be able to obtain a regulated and, therefore, pure supply of a substance that they would previously have obtained from the unregulated black market. This is unequivocally a safer situation for them and is a basic consumer right and expectation.

Secondly, they would not be criminalised for possession of a drug other than alcohol, tobacco and caffeine. This means they would not suffer the serious and often life-altering consequences of being involved in the criminal justice system due to the possession of a drug of choice.

The current policy regime maximises the danger for the young in relation to the use of drugs both licit and illicit. A legal and regulated supply of all substances is the only sensible circumstance and provides for the safest environment in relation to the young and their use of recreational drugs.

WHAT IS NEEDED FOR CHANGE?

For change to occur on a fundamental level, two basic actions would end the GESICC. Firstly, abolition of the three 'drug control' conventions administered by the United Nations. These are the instruments in international law that obligate signatories to participate in the GESICC. They lay the foundation for the defining of a minority for criminalisation and subsequent economic utilisation by the listing of psychoactive substances except for alcohol, tobacco and caffeine. The United Nations must not be involved in administering a policy that is founded upon the criminalisation and subsequent economic utilisation of a minority.

Secondly, abolition of the Controlled Substances Act in the U.S. and its international equivalents. Each participating country has an instrument in law that facilitates the criminalisation of a minority so that they become an economic resource and able to be utilised in order to enable financial gain and political advantage. This is achieved by the exclusion from the Acts of three substances: alcohol, tobacco and caffeine.

There must be no instruments in law that provide for the criminalisation of associations with any recreational psychoactive substance whether that be possession, use or lawful supply activities.

IMPEDIMENTS TO CHANGE

That the GESICC has to cease is beyond debate. Utilising a minority for financial and political gain is obviously unacceptable. The cruelty, resultant suffering and corruption created by the policy is immense. The primary impediment to the cessation of the GESICC is the loss of money by those currently profiting from it and the subsequent economic ramifications such as loss of employment and profits. These events would in turn have political consequences.

Those who have no wish for the policy to end due to the particular loss of advantage they would sustain are able to be categorised under two general headings.

THOSE SUSTAINED FINANCIALLY BY THE POLICY

These people see the cessation of the policy primarily in terms of loss of money either from the removal or reduction of public money distributed or the collapse of the black market in drugs other than alcohol, tobacco and caffeine. This loss of income would be felt particularly amongst sectors such as the criminal justice system and governmental and non-governmental welfare and advocacy, for example.

THOSE SUSTAINED POLITICALLY BY THE POLICY

There is one fundamental form of political advantage offered by the GESICC that politicians would be highly reluctant to relinquish. This is their portrayal as providing protection to the populace from a threat to health and welfare.

The political advantage is attained courtesy of a simple formula: politicians falsely represent themselves as providing protection to the populace from harm due to drug use. This gives them apparent justification to distribute public money in order to seemingly engage with and control the contrived threat thereby allowing them to create a substantial amount of economic activity. This distribution of funds provides political advantage due to the recipients of the money voting to continue its distribution.

Those who mistakenly believe that the threat is legitimate also vote for the continuation of the strategy. It is basic human nature to be fearful of an apparent threat to health and welfare and, therefore, highly supportive of anyone purporting to provide protection from the supposed threat. The strategy is successful beyond imagination as evidenced by the fact that the GESICC has been in existence for many decades.

Regarding the possibility of political impetus for change and the ways it might come about, politicians will never admit that they have enabled a policy that utilises a minority for financial and political gain by selectively criminalising them. To admit to the true nature of the 'War on Drugs' would be extremely damaging in terms of the public's perception of their governance structures and is an action that is politically unfeasible.

It must end, however, and only open and honest discussion and, thereby, genuine acknowledgement of the issues will allow this to happen. Understanding of the deceptive and malevolent nature of the present policy regime is critical to initiating the process of change.

HONESTY ABOUT THE DISTRIBUTION
OF PUBLIC MONEY

It would be ideal for society (including government and the populace) to be honest about the distribution of public money and its role in the economy. It is reasonable to say that one of the greatest impediments to ending the GESICC would be the reduction of public money flowing from government and the subsequent loss of employment and profits.

An example would be that if all prisoners in the U.S. with a 'drug' conviction were to be released, federal prison populations, in particular, would be dramatically reduced. This would have major ramifications for the workforce and those involved in supporting the prisons. The political difficulties arising from a situation such as this would be substantial.

Fundamentally, the issue in relation to public money being distributed to prevent a degree of humanitarian crisis due to unemployment is the creation and acceptance of an honest and equitable welfare system. The GESICC is, in terms of public money distributed, a welfare system that is deceptively justified as a response to a threat to health and welfare. This false justification allows political administrations to imply that they are distributing public money for a worthwhile and necessary purpose rather than purely as a response to the inability of society to provide people with sufficient employment opportunities.

The key to ending the GESICC in terms of the distribution of public money will be putting in place a strategy that sees money allocated on a basis that is not related to the criminalisation and exploitation of a minority as has been the case for the last fifty years. The distribution of public money should never be based upon a response to intentionally-created crime and, therefore, a strategy that constitutes a blatant human-rights abuse. The distribution of public money must be on an equitable basis that does not involve the oppression and economic utilisation of people.

CHANGE ITSELF

The salient issue is how change can be brought about in a way that is achievable on an economic and political basis. There are, in genuine terms, only two alternatives available for the future of the GESICC.

The first one is unacceptable: this is the continuation of the atrocity. This is the option favoured by politicians of all persuasions and those profiting from the situation. Many who offer welfare and advocacy services appear content with the continuation of the policy despite the regime's inherent inequity and oppression. They generally appear to support the continuation of the categorisation of people by the Controlled Substances Act and its equivalents which facilitates the provision of interventions such as mandated 'treatment' that enable the distribution of public money.

The policy change advocated for by those who appear content with the GESICC continuing but who represent themselves as being compassionate is decriminalisation of possession. However, this is not substantive change to the regime. Under decriminalisation, the penalties for possession are modified and decreased in severity but the fundamental basis remains: associations with controlled substances constitute an offence and, therefore, a minority is defined for economic utilisation.

The continuation of the GESICC would resign the world to a perpetual and ingrained state of intentionally-created crime that grows in vigour with each increase in public money devoted to responding to it. As has occurred since its inception in the early 1970s, each increase in the number of people reliant upon it makes it more difficult to end due to the political ramifications involved. Consequently, the suffering increases and the fabric of society is eroded accordingly.

The criminalised minority becomes more oppressed and impoverished and the people benefiting become more reliant upon carrying out the oppression. Such a situation is conducive to the guaranteed incremental degradation of society and prevents us from having harmonious and productive structures upon which to base our existence.

The second circumstance is a genuine end to the policy regime. The nature of a strategy that would enable a genuine cessation is the matter that would require resolution. As previously noted, it hinges largely upon how to deal with the loss of public money allocated and money generated by the black market in drugs other than alcohol, tobacco and caffeine.

Along with a legal supply of all psychoactive substances, there is one obvious way of promptly halting the atrocity without causing immediate and politically unpalatable unemployment due to the withdrawal of public money. This would be to cease the activities currently undertaken as part of the policy such as investigating, arresting, fining, imprisoning and mandated treatment etc., and simply maintain the funding of those previously involved in these activities.

In other words, maintain the funding and, thereby, the employment of the people who were involved in exploiting the criminalised minority even though they would no longer be engaged in these activities. This strategy would allow for the cessation of the GESICC without causing substantial economic, social and political ramifications due to the withdrawal of public money.

However confronting it appears initially, the strategy of maintaining the funding and, thereby, the employment of those who would no longer be engaged in their previous activities is at least worthy of consideration as a means of scaling back and ultimately halting the atrocity that has plagued the world for half a century.

Taking this step would allow time to consider the best methods for redeploying the people previously employed by the GESICC and to formulate a system providing for the distribution of public money that is not based upon the criminalisation and subsequent economic utilisation of a minority. This strategy would of course lay bare the obscene nature of what has been happening for the last fifty years which has simply been the facilitation of political advantage by the criminalisation and subsequent economic utilisation of a minority under the pretext of protecting health and welfare. There perhaps cannot be a more damning indictment on humanity than an economic system reliant for its existence on the oppression of a minority.

Society would become much more equitable and peaceful due to a minority no longer being criminalised and subsequently utilised for political and economic purposes. The opportunity would exist for the implementation of mechanisms that would see public money distributed on a basis that does not involve the criminalisation and subsequent exploitation of any person.

In relation to the cessation of the black market in drugs other than alcohol, tobacco and caffeine, the worldwide economy would adapt and money from taxation of the legal and regulated supply of previously illicit substances would provide increased legitimate income for government.

To conclude this section, I would like to document and discuss briefly the consequences of the GESICC being discontinued. Firstly, as a result of the massive global economic system based upon intentionally-created crime ceasing, there would be an unprecedented reduction in crime. Worldwide, a large number of people would no longer be committing a crime simply by being involved in the supply, possession or use of drugs other than alcohol, tobacco and caffeine.

Those who happen to use a drug other than alcohol, tobacco and caffeine would be able to go about their lives without being arrested, legally processed, fined, imprisoned, subjected to mandated interventions described as treatment and brutalised in general. Their lives would no longer be chaotic due to the effects of being criminalised in respect of their personal drug use.

They would have access to a legal, regulated and quality assured supply of their drug of choice as do the users of alcohol, tobacco, and caffeine. Their health and welfare would no longer be compromised due to an unregulated supply of the substances.

Worldwide, hundreds of thousands of people would no longer be imprisoned. In the U.S. alone, tens of billions of dollars annually would be available to be allocated for the betterment of society rather than being distributed on the basis of the criminalisation and subsequent economic utilisation of a minority.

Wars would no longer be fought to control the production of drugs other than alcohol, tobacco and caffeine. Societies that were previously ravaged by violence associated with control of illicit drug markets would have the opportunity to return to a peaceful existence in this respect.

These are just some of the things that would happen due to the cessation of a worldwide economic system based upon intentionally-created crime and enabled by the criminalisation of a minority. An occurrence that would be similar in many respects to the ending of a world war. A situation to look forward to with great anticipation.

CONCLUSION

The intention of this book is to explain the true nature of an obscene worldwide phenomenon that has as its basis the criminalisation of a minority in order to facilitate financial gain and political advantage. Only when the true nature of the policy regime is known and accepted can a genuine discussion about it take place. In conclusion, I will briefly reiterate the important points and the fundamental message conveyed in this book.

The phenomenon known as the 'War on Drugs' is portrayed as a strategy to prevent and minimise harm due to the use of psychoactive substances or what are commonly referred to as 'drugs'. The fundamental mechanism employed by the policy to apparently provide for deterrence and punishment in relation to associations with psychoactive substances is the imposition of criminal sanctions.

The fundamental document whose purpose is portrayed as classifying substances according to their capacity for harm and, thereby, allowing for the imposition of criminal sanctions on those who associate with the drugs is the Single Convention on Narcotic Drugs, 1961. Each participating country has an act based upon it. However, the drugs alcohol, tobacco and caffeine are not included in these documents and, therefore, associations with these three drugs are not deemed to be unlawful. Consequently, the suppliers and users of these three drugs are not criminalised due to an association with the substances.

The generally inferred rationale for the policy is the prevention and minimisation of harm to health and welfare due to the use of psychoactive substances. However, those involved in possession, use, and lawful supply of the two most dangerous drugs in existence (alcohol and tobacco) and caffeine are not criminalised. Obviously, the policy regime is not genuine regarding its apparent purpose of protecting health and welfare in relation to the use of psychoactive substances.

So, the policy represented as a war on drugs is not concerned with preventing and minimising drug-related harm. What then, are its actual intentions? The purpose of the policy is simply and unequivocally the intentional creation and maintenance of crime in order to provide the basis for economic activity that delivers financial gain and, consequently, political advantage.

The intentionally-created crime provides the basis for two primary outcomes both of which are politically desirable and enormously successful as witnessed by the continuance and vibrancy of the policy over a period of many decades. Firstly, the distribution of vast amounts of public money to facilitate a response to the intentionally-created crime. Secondly, a lucrative worldwide black market in drugs other than alcohol, tobacco and caffeine.

The phenomenon is founded upon the intentional creation of crime and, thereby, criminals. The crime is solely a person's association with drugs other than alcohol, tobacco and caffeine. These people are the resource for an industry of enforcement and 'welfare' activities funded by public money and as suppliers and consumers they facilitate the extraordinarily lucrative worldwide black market in illicit drugs.

It is solely an economic and, therefore, politically advantageous policy based upon intentionally-created crime. Nothing more and nothing less. It is not related in any way to preventing and minimising harm due to the use of psychoactive substances of any kind.

Following are two fundamental statements of fact that illustrate the situation regarding the policy regime that criminalises a minority as defined by their associations with drugs other than alcohol, tobacco and caffeine for the purpose of enabling financial gain and political advantage. The statements are unable to be disputed in any credible manner.

*The only way the policy regime referred to
as the 'War on Drugs' could be a genuine strategy to
prevent and minimise harm due to the use of psychoactive
substances is the criminalisation of associations with
all drugs including alcohol, tobacco and caffeine.*

*The only way the policy regime referred to
as the 'War on Drugs' could not be an intentionally
selective crime-creation and maintenance scheme is its
cessation or the criminalisation of associations with
all drugs including alcohol, tobacco and caffeine.*

To reiterate, the fundamental deception employed is that the policy is concerned with the control of drug use in order to prevent and minimise harm to health and welfare. Obviously, the policy is not concerned in any way with preventing or minimising harm due to drug use as associations with alcohol, tobacco and caffeine are not criminalised as are associations with other drugs.

The fundamental basis of the policy regime is the intentional creation of crime in order to facilitate financial gain and political advantage. The mechanism in law that enables the intentional and selective creation of crime and, thereby, criminals is the classifying of psychoactive substances except for alcohol, tobacco and caffeine. The foundation document that performs this selective classification is the Single Convention on Narcotic Drugs, 1961. Each country participating in the GESICC has its own version of the document.

The policy is politically successful due in large part to its portrayal as protecting people from a threat to health and welfare and politically achievable due to its oppressive and exploitative mechanisms being imposed solely upon a minority. It achieves political advantage due in part to the distribution of substantial amounts of public money which creates economic activity manifesting as jobs and profits. It is particularly lucrative for the criminal justice system as it provides a perpetual supply of criminals to investigate, arrest, process, fine, imprison, refer for mandated interventions described as treatment, etc. This activity is funded by public money and employs a substantial number of people.

All the public money allocated, the money created by the black market in illicit drugs and the resulting political advantage is based upon the inequitable and abhorrent treatment of a minority. A human resource created by selective criminalisation based solely upon associations with drugs other than alcohol, tobacco and caffeine.

The world is entrenched in an intentionally created and maintained system of crime and oppression based upon the criminalisation of a minority. It was initiated many decades ago by the United States and is administered by the United Nations. It results in oppression and cruelty on a worldwide basis including mass imprisonment, wars in order to control the production of opium and violence and murder related to control of the black market in illicit substances.

There will hopefully come a time when the human race becomes civilised enough to not allow a situation in which people prey upon each other by way of a contrived obscenity that has been described here as the GESICC or that is commonly referred to as the 'War on Drugs'. It is abhorrent almost beyond description and is a manifestation of the worst of human behaviour.

No society that participates can dare call itself civilised or humane. It is a completely intentional and self-perpetuating phenomenon that bears witness to man's inhumanity to man. For the past fifty years the phenomenon has defined mankind as being brutal and mercenary.

But it does not have to be. The policy regime is completely intentional and, therefore, it is completely within our capabilities to bring about a cessation of the atrocity. There is only one appropriate course of action which is simply to stop it.

EPILOGUE

I would like to list some realisations that I have come to during my time being immersed in the subject of psychoactive substance use and the legal and economic constructs associated with it. To come to an understanding of the motives and behaviour of people in relation to the treatment of their fellow man has required a process involving persistence and analysis. Following are some points of significance that I have become aware of during my journey:

• The so-called 'War on Drugs' is not related in any way to the prevention and minimisation of drug-related harm. It is about the attainment of financial gain and political advantage and is based upon the criminalisation and subsequent economic utilisation of a minority as defined by their associations with drugs other than alcohol, tobacco and caffeine.

The fundamental instrument that enables the worldwide phenomenon is the Single Convention on Narcotic Drugs, 1961. Each participating country has its own document in law based upon it: in the U.S. it is the

Controlled Substances Act. As long as these Acts exclude alcohol, tobacco and caffeine, they can be nothing other than mechanisms of selective crime creation and, therefore, instruments of oppression. The exclusion of alcohol, tobacco and caffeine is the fundamental circumstance that defines the Acts as instruments whose sole purpose is to categorise those who are to be utilised for financial gain and political advantage.

• There is a massive worldwide industrial complex based upon the aforementioned laws. Those sectors who may profit from the oppression of others include but are not limited to law enforcement, the legal system, the prison industry (both public and private), academia, governmental and non-governmental welfare and advocacy and those who supply and support them. And of course, politicians. None of these people will, under any circumstances, tell the truth about the atrocity that may sustain them to some degree and some will go to great lengths to conceal the true nature of the phenomenon.

As a generalisation, those who benefit from the policy regime appear happy for it to continue regardless of it being based upon the inequitable treatment of people. There is a multitude of people and organisations that benefit financially from the regime, and employment provided by the strategy is substantial and far-reaching within society. Those who are sustained by the regime appear content with continuing to receive the public money distributed under the policy, the commercial advantage afforded to their particular industry or the income from the black market in drugs other than alcohol, tobacco and caffeine.

• There is not and never has been any evidence that overdose of heroin and, therefore, its primary active metabolite morphine results in harmful compromise or cessation of breathing.

• The process that most often leads to injury or death due to compromise or cessation of breathing in relation to the use of central nervous system depressant drugs is profound and disabling sedation leading to airway obstruction and resultant asphyxiation. The sedation is commonly brought about by combinations of depressant drugs and this situation is universally and incorrectly referred to as 'overdose'.

• Advocacy and welfare groups and others purporting to be concerned about the oppressive measures of what is represented as a war on drugs generally call for 'drug-law reform'. This is represented as a way of making the policy regime less cruel and oppressive on those affected by it. In reality though, the concept described by some as 'drug-law reform' is highly deceptive and based upon retaining the selective criminalisation of people albeit with minor alterations to give the impression that substantive changes have been made. The strategy is dishonest from three main perspectives.

Firstly, the term 'drug law' implies that the policy regime is a valid and genuine intervention by governments to prevent and minimise harm due to the use of psychoactive substances and, therefore, should remain in place. This of course, is incorrect. What is represented as 'drug law' is not related in any way to minimising drug-related harm as it does not address associations with alcohol, tobacco and caffeine. The term 'drug law' is simply a deceptive synonym for the policy regime represented as a war on drugs and is not related to the control of drug use or drug-related harm.

Secondly, the call for reform implies that 'drug law' has been badly formulated or applied in an incorrect or over-zealous manner that has resulted in it being unjust and oppressive in nature and that it should be modified so as not to be so oppressive on those affected by it. This is a fallacy, as the GESICC is a wholly intentional strategy based upon the criminalisation and subsequent economic utilisation of a minority in order to enable financial gain and political advantage. It is an entirely malevolent construct and cannot be fixed or modified in any way to make it equitable and fair.

The third deception is that many of those who are apparently calling for modification to 'drug law' on the basis that it is oppressive and cruel presumably have an interest in it continuing due to being sustained by the public money distributed under it. For the distribution of money to continue, the minority must continue to be defined for criminalisation and, therefore, liable to various interventions such as mandated 'treatment'.

• Decriminalisation is predominately the specific modification to 'drug law' advocated for by those wishing to be perceived as compassionate towards the people oppressed and economically utilised under it. Decriminalisation is portrayed as being a substantive change to policy relating to the treatment of those who associate with drugs other than alcohol, tobacco and caffeine.

It is, however, merely a lessening of the penalties for possession. An association with drugs other than alcohol, tobacco and caffeine involving supply, possession or use continues to be classified as an offence. Essentially, the concept of decriminalisation is a convenient illusion that allows for the continued defining of a minority for economic utilisation as provided for by the Controlled Substances Act and its international equivalents.

For those funded by public money, decriminalisation is an advantageous strategy from three perspectives. Firstly, advocating for it portrays them as being compassionate and progressive in relation to those who are oppressed and economically utilised under the GESICC. Secondly, advocating for decriminalisation provides support for the continuation of the underlying policy regime and, therefore, the defining of a minority for the purpose of economic utilisation including interventions such as opioid substitution therapy.

Finally, by advocating for decriminalisation, these organisations are not defying government and are therefore not endangering their funding. Under decriminalisation, the fundamental structures of the GESICC that are desired by governments remain in place: the selective criminalisation of people in order to enable financial and political gain and the criminalisation of the supply of drugs other than alcohol, tobacco and caffeine.

• The deceptive use of language in order to conceal complicity is something that I have become very familiar with. Terms are used to blatantly disavow the existence of the aggressive oppression of the GESICC and misrepresent the cause of people's misfortune as being their personal choice to use drugs other than alcohol, tobacco and caffeine. Invariably such terms are used by those involved in the welfare and advocacy sectors and, therefore, sustained by public money. I would like to use one term as an example. The use of this term has become common in the U.S. especially by welfare organisations to describe their client base. The term is 'people who use drugs'. This term is fundamentally misleading and dishonest as it serves to categorise those who use drugs other than alcohol, tobacco and caffeine as a specific and unique segment of society via the false assertion that they are the only members of society that use psychoactive substances. The term implies they are a deviant and problematic cohort and, therefore, deserving of special treatment by the state.

The term actually describes those people who are criminalised as defined by their associations with drugs other than alcohol, tobacco and caffeine for the purpose of enabling their utilisation on an economic basis. The term actually describes those people whose lives are intentionally made chaotic for the purpose of exploiting them through the imposition of various interventions.

Use of the term suggests that 'people who use drugs' are a group of people who are, due to their apparently imprudent personal choices relating to substance use, somehow unique in relation to a requirement for welfare-related interventions. It actually describes a segment of society that often becomes the clients of welfare organisations due solely to the consequences of being criminalised and economically utilised rather than because of any health-related issue due to the use of a particular substance.

There are a number of terms used by the welfare and advocacy sectors which communicate the impression that they believe the policy represented as a war on drugs is unjust and oppressive but which also clearly signal their failure to be honest about its true nature and effects on people. Terms include 'drug policy', 'drug-law reform', 'evidence-based policy', 'harm reduction' and, as just discussed, 'people who use drugs'.

The welfare and advocacy organisations using terms such as these will not under any circumstances acknowledge that the criminalisation of people as defined by their associations with illicit drugs is solely for the purpose of enabling their exploitation.

The willingness of some in the welfare and advocacy sectors to use deceptive terms to disavow the true nature of what is represented as a war on drugs has a clear basis in self-interest. Some organisations derive a degree of benefit from the selective criminalisation of people as it provides them with a human resource to provide government-funded interventions for.

• In reference to the intervention referred to as 'harm reduction', it is represented as an altruistic strategy to reduce the harm caused by the use of illicit substances when the person involved is intent on using the drug. The term is used to imply that the use of illicit drugs is somehow uniquely and inherently dangerous and, thereby, to justify the imposition of apparently necessary interventions to minimise the harm caused by use of the substances. These interventions are funded by public money, employ a substantial number of people and it is deemed unnecessary to be preoccupied with imposing them on the users of the two most dangerous drugs in existence: alcohol and tobacco.

In relation to those who associate with illicit drugs, however, use of the substances is often not the predominant cause of harm. The harm sustained by these people is due largely to them being intentionally criminalised and, subsequently, economically utilised. The harm can be as a result of forced involvement in the criminal justice system that can include arrest, fines, imprisonment and coerced interventions described as treatment. It can include the denial of housing, insurance, government benefits and employment, for example, due to the existence of a criminal record. The harm caused by these interventions results solely from the criminalisation of supply and possession of people's drugs of choice.

This harm is intentionally imposed upon people by governments simply because it facilitates financial gain and political advantage. This is the harm and it is falsely attributed to the use of substances other than alcohol, tobacco and caffeine as a way of justifying and perpetuating the policies that enable it.

- The GESICC has a significantly negative impact on the environment. One obvious and horrifying example is the aerial fumigation of coca crops in South America. This strategy had a catastrophic effect on the environment and on the health of its inhabitants. The use of electricity to provide light for clandestine indoor cannabis crops generates carbon emissions that largely would not be created in a world of legal and regulated supply as the crops would often be grown outdoors. Clandestine crops also contribute to deforestation due to them being situated in forested areas in order to prevent their detection.

- The existence of the GESICC proves unequivocally that in terms of policy designed to protect human rights, if there is anything of this nature in place in a country that subscribes to the regime, it is fundamentally powerless and ineffectual in nature. The GESICC is a blatant and gratuitous worldwide human-rights abuse and for it to exist there must also be a complete absence of effective laws to protect people from inequitable and abusive treatment. The existence of the GESICC makes a complete mockery of anything portrayed as being a mechanism to protect human-rights.

- In relation to police and specialist enforcement agencies, the GESICC has them involving in the criminal justice system people who are not negatively affecting public order and who are merely associating with a drug of choice. This is something many police and the majority in society do on a daily basis and which is considered by them as a normal activity and a basic entitlement to be taken for granted.

Essentially, the role of police is to protect and maintain public order for the good of society. However, their involvement in prosecuting the GESICC transforms their role to include inequitable treatment of their fellow man and carrying out interventions that they would deem unacceptable if imposed upon themselves or the majority in society. This is not consistent with what should be their duty: to protect and maintain public order in a fair and equitable manner.

A situation exists worldwide in which enforcement agencies actively engage in inequitable and aggressive behaviour towards their fellow man under the banner of a policy regime that is falsely represented as existing to protect health and welfare. This situation denies them respect and results in them being feared and despised by the segment of society involved when they intervene in this regard.

• In relation to politicians, their role is portrayed as management of our existence so that we can live a life that is sustainable and governed by rules that promote peaceful relationships with our fellow man. Universally and worldwide, however, politicians enable, maintain and misrepresent the nature of a system of intentionally-created crime that involves the brutal and aggressive oppression of a minority.

Politicians do this solely to enable the attainment of financial gain and political advantage. They have no right to do this and it defines our existence as being governed by mercenary and uncivilised behaviour that has persisted for half a century and shows no genuine indication of coming to an end. No politician is prepared to be honest about what is happening and this indicates that an end to the atrocity will be protracted and difficult. But it must end as it is simply not acceptable for it to continue. We cannot continue to have a system of worldwide economic activity based upon oppression.

• At times it is difficult to come to terms with the duplicity that some people are capable of and the constant and shameless lying that takes place in order to disavow the mistreatment of people and, thereby, to assist in perpetuating this behaviour in the pursuit of financial gain and political advantage. Also encountered on a constant basis is hypocrisy. The willingness of people to apply standards of behaviour to others that they would not accept being imposed upon themselves in order to achieve personal gain is a hallmark of the policy represented as a war on drugs.

My journey has been one in which the common factor encountered, unfortunately, is the willingness of people to oppress and exploit their fellow man in order to enable financial gain and political advantage. The behaviour is perpetual and multi-faceted. The number of people who profit from and are sustained to some degree by the GESICC is alarming and their silence in relation to the phenomenon that forms the basis for some or all of their activities is truly disturbing.

There is no limit to the cruelty that many people will impose upon others in order to enable financial gain under the banner of the GESICC. It is frightening and not conducive to a situation in which the human race could ever be described as being truly civilised. Until we as a society engage in an honest and candid conversation about what is happening, the atrocity will continue and along with it the completely avoidable oppression and resultant suffering that has plagued the world for half a century.

SUPPLEMENTARY CONTENT

I would like to discuss some subjects that are relevant and significant in relation to the content of this book and, in doing so, provide an open and truthful account of the particular topics.

HEROIN AND OTHER OPIOIDS

I wish to speak in an informal manner about the drug that is incorrectly portrayed as being the most dangerous based upon the assertion that an overdose of the substance can result in impaired breathing. I have detailed the relevant points in relation to heroin not being dangerous in overdose in the first chapter and have referenced a modern study that unequivocally proves this in a clinical and controlled setting.

There are also some general points of interest regarding opioids that I would like to convey in order to help and inform people: those who currently use opioids, those who are contemplating using them and parents who are concerned about the safety of their children should they use the substances. Most importantly, I will reiterate and expand upon critical information previously given in relation to the process that can lead to adverse events caused by combinations of central nervous system depressant drugs including opioids.

A very small number of people use opioids for non-medical purposes. I respect their decision to do this just as I respect the decision of those who choose to use drugs such as alcohol or tobacco. Opioids are merely one substance amongst many that people take on a recreational basis for their subjectively positive effects on the central nervous system.

People should have access to opioid medications for purposes such as the treatment of pain and conditions such as breathlessness in the palliative care setting. People should have access to opioids, particularly morphine, at the end of life. Opioids are invaluable in easing the discomfort commonly encountered at this difficult time.

When I was working in the mental health field in a community based residential facility in approximately 2006, I had the opportunity to assist a long-time heroin user. This man gave an account of his life as a mechanical design engineer and often spoke about some of the projects he had been involved in over the course of his career. One day I mentioned the subject of heroin overdose as I was interested in his experience and knowledge on the subject. He turned to me with an expression of slight annoyance and said that when he overdosed he became nauseous and suffered a headache. He was obviously aware from personal experience that the ingestion of an amount of heroin in excess of that normally taken was not dangerous.

This was an important point in my journey of trying to get to the truth through an almost impenetrable wall of propaganda and misinformation. From that point on, all my research and experiences from working in the alcohol and other drug and healthcare sectors led me to some realisations supported by evidence and common sense. So accordingly, I will briefly reiterate some fundamental points relating to opioid use and, more specifically, heroin.

Heroin is considered a pro-drug for morphine. This means it is essentially a delivery system for morphine. Morphine is a central nervous system depressant drug that is not toxic to the body and has the peerless ability to ease pain. It is the 'gold standard' for the treatment of serious pain and is indispensable in this regard. It causes nausea in the majority of people who use it. With consistent use it causes persistent and severe constipation in most people. These two factors make it a highly undesirable drug to use on a recreational basis other than for a very small minority of people.

There is no evidence that morphine, even in substantial overdose, causes harmful compromise or cessation of breathing by affecting the body's autonomic (automatic) control of breathing. There is indisputable evidence that substantial overdose of morphine does not present a danger regarding breathing.

For the safe use of heroin, morphine and other opioids, it is important that dangerous combinations of central nervous system depressant drugs are avoided. The substances that can contribute to a dangerous situation in combination with opioids (or with each other) are alcohol, benzodiazepines, barbiturates and other sedative-hypnotic medications, for example.

The process initiated by a combination of depressant drugs including or not including opioids that can lead to injury or death is profound and disabling sedation leading to airway obstruction and asphyxiation (oxygen starvation).

A person sedated to unconsciousness by a combination of central nervous system depressant drugs and not able to be roused cannot control the position of their head and, therefore, their neck and jaw. Accordingly, structures in their throat and/or vomit may block or impede the passage of air to and from their lungs and result in a situation of inadequate oxygen intake that can lead to brain injury or death.

I want to state in the strongest possible terms that this information does not apply solely to the use of opioids. It is critical that those taking any central nervous system depressant drug in combination with others are aware of this process and its possible consequences. For those using depressant drugs, the avoidance of dangerous combinations of the substances is of paramount importance.

MULTIPLE-DRUG TOXICITY
INVOLVING OPIOIDS: AN OBSERVATION

Taking opioids in the absence of hazardous combinations of central nervous system depressant drugs is not problematic apart from nausea and constipation. Based upon the evidence I have seen and on anecdotal accounts, the events and basic mechanisms leading to a situation of dangerous sedation due to substance use when opioids are involved are, frequently, as follows.

The person already has one or more substances in their body such as alcohol, benzodiazepines or barbiturates, for example, that has or have the ability to induce sedation: predominantly this will involve the 'GABA' system. Gamma-Aminobutyric acid (GABA) is a major inhibitory neurotransmitter and acts to reduce excitability of nerve cells. The presence of other substances may be because the person has an irregular supply of opioids, is seeking an increased euphoric effect or is taking a medication, for example.

They then introduce an opioid to their body. The presence of two or more different substances that act on similar or dissimilar neuronal systems in the brain can result in profound and disabling sedation. This sedation can lead to airway obstruction and asphyxiation. As I have emphasised repeatedly, the hazards of mixing depressant drugs does not apply solely to the use of opioids.

There is a paucity of information relating to multiple-drug toxicity as governments and those funded by them are committed to the false narrative of opioids causing hazardous compromise of breathing by affecting the body's autonomic control of respiration. This provides the basis upon which to scaremonger about and to malign opioids which assists governments in perpetuating the oppression and economic utilisation of those who use the substances.

Despite awareness of the danger of multiple-drug toxicity, governments and their agents, the media and others persist in describing adverse events involving combinations of depressant drugs and, especially, those involving opioids as 'overdoses'. This course of action is deceptive, dishonest and dangerous.

FOR PARENTS

COMPARATIVE SCENARIOS

One of the fundamental tools employed by those wishing to perpetuate the GESICC is the creation of fear in the minds of parents regarding the welfare of their children in relation to illicit substances. With respect to the GESICC, however, it is critical for parents to be aware of two points. Firstly, that the policy is not concerned with the health and welfare of young people regarding 'drugs' and, secondly, the intention of the policy in relation to the young if they happen to use substances other than alcohol, tobacco and caffeine is economic exploitation.

As an illustration of the consequences of the current crime-creation and maintenance scheme and its effect on people, it is appropriate to provide and discuss two hypothetical scenarios in order that parents may consider the effects on a person if that person happened to be their child.

The first scenario is applicable to the current situation and is a common outcome as dictated by the policy of criminalising people as defined by their associations with certain substances in order to facilitate financial and political gain. It is followed by a scenario depicting a person's life when that person is not criminalised as defined by an association with a drug of choice.

148

The substance used for illustration purposes is morphine simply because as a result of them comprising a tiny minority in society, opioid users are, as a group, treated in the most aggressive and oppressive manner under the current policy regime.

Consider a young person who has found that morphine is the drug that suits them as alcohol, tobacco or caffeine may suit others. They are part of a very small minority in society that as a personal choice takes the substance on a recreational basis. They have a desire to regularly use the substance even though it has troublesome side effects such as nausea and constipation. Apart from these universal side effects, it does not present a serious risk to their health.

In fact, they may prefer the drug because of its low toxicity compared to other drugs such as alcohol or tobacco. In relation to the use of a substance for its psychoactive effects, they are engaging in the same activity as do so many others in society. They are merely using a different drug to those used by the majority.

They may have a chronic or emerging mental disorder for which they find morphine gives some relief or perhaps it helps them deal with memories of traumatic circumstances they may have encountered. Or, they may simply enjoy the effects of the drug as so many others enjoy the effects of alcohol.

However, due to them being part of a minority (opioid users) and, therefore, subject to being oppressed and exploited, the supply and possession of their drug of choice is subject to criminal sanctions. They must obtain their substance from the black market and, consequently, manufacture of the drug is not regulated. Obtaining their drug of choice from the black market contributes to making their lifestyle chaotic as they are not able to go to a retail outlet and obtain a legal and regulated product at a time and place of their choosing. A significant part of each day must be devoted to obtaining the substance from an unreliable source.

They may, as is so often the case, be ostracised by their parents and others for using a substance that is deemed unacceptable due to a lack of understanding of its nature, the real reasons for its illegality and because it is the drug of a minority.

They may find themselves being arrested, charged and convicted for possession of an illicit drug. This has a profound effect on their lives from this point on. Their ability to secure employment and, thereby, housing and other essentials of life is compromised. They begin to struggle in life because their criminal record makes employment difficult to obtain. If they resort to supplying the substance in order to have a source of income and are subsequently convicted of this, their troubles will be intensified as supply is treated more harshly than possession by the criminal justice system.

Their peers who use alcohol as their drug of choice are free to make their way through life and can use their drug without consequence from the criminal justice system. They are not defined by their association with a drug of choice as being an economic resource to be exploited.

Due to being unable to gain employment, the person is forced to embark on a lifestyle of homelessness interspersed with securing shelter from charitable organisations. Their health suffers due to the chaotic lifestyle enforced upon them.

Along the way they are incarcerated and become further embittered and despondent. This experience intensifies the emotional troubles they have due to being generally mistreated and rejected by society.

They become overwhelmed by feelings of hopelessness after ten or so years of being hunted by enforcement agencies and treated as if they are a liability and less worthy of existence than others. They tend to combine drugs more often and in a more risky manner due to having an irregular supply of their drug of choice.

One day they combine alcohol and heroin, become profoundly sedated due to the combination of drugs and succumb to asphyxiation due to airway obstruction. This

151

occurs in an alley in a suburban area of a major city after they had travelled to the location due to it being a known black-market source of their drug of choice.

The young person's mother is subsequently recruited by the media and appears in press articles often posing beside a picture of her child. The articles insinuate that illicit drugs were the sole factor that led to the downfall and death of the person. No consideration is given to the fact that they were criminalised as defined by an association with a drug of choice and that their difficulties were almost entirely caused by this criminalisation and subsequent exploitation.

This is a scenario brought about purely by the criminalisation of young people as a way of achieving political advantage through financial gain. A ruthless and completely intentional system of oppression and exploitation achievable simply because those utilised are part of a minority and, therefore, vulnerable to having conditions enforced upon them that would never be imposed upon the majority in society.

Contrast the preceding scenario with the following situation involving the same young person under circumstances in which they are not criminalised as defined by an association with a drug of choice and are therefore not economically exploited under a system of intentionally-created crime.

The person has an experience with several drugs during their adolescence and finds that morphine is the one that satisfies their needs best. They choose to take the drug even though the nausea and constipation are troublesome at times. They learn to live with and minimise these side effects as time goes on.

They purchase a supply of pharmaceutical grade heroin at a licensed recreational drug outlet three times a week when they attain the age of eighteen years. They are educated on the danger of combining central nervous system depressant drugs at drug education classes throughout their secondary schooling and use this knowledge to keep themselves safe.

They use the drug most days of the week and it rarely interferes with their educational or employment obligations. The person's parents accept their child's drug use reluctantly but are pleased that they take a responsible approach to the substance and its use. They are grateful that their child is not criminalised as defined by their drug use as happened in the twentieth and part of the twenty-first centuries.

The person secures ongoing employment after completing a relevant course of education and finds a partner who accepts their drug use. The two settle down, are fortunate to be able to buy a house and some years later have two children whom they raise successfully.

The person ceases the regular use of morphine in their mid-forties after tiring of the constipation. They remember the way the substance made them feel and the relief it gave them from troublesome thoughts. They have, however, come to a certain peace with their memories and the negatives associated with the use of morphine have come to outweigh the positives. They continue to use it on an occasional basis for the rest of their life.

The couple continues to live without the imposition of criminalisation as defined by the use of a particular drug. Their lives contain the same trials and tribulations as others endure and they are able to overcome them in the same manner that others do.

This account of two scenarios attempts to communicate to parents that the policy represented as a war on drugs is not a mechanism to protect your children or anyone else from drug-related harm. It is simply an economic system based upon intentionally-created crime and facilitated by the criminalisation of a minority including young people. It is not about drugs or drug-related harm. It is about financial gain and the political advantage arising from this.

In relation to the use of psychoactive substances by young people from the perspective of their parents, the policy regime provides for two main circumstances.

Firstly, the unrestricted use and promotion of alcohol which is the most dangerous drug for the young. It is commonly and routinely associated with violence, unsafe sexual activity and risk-taking behaviours such as dangerous driving due to its disinhibitory effects. The Centers for Disease Control and Prevention estimate that in the United States, *"Excessive drinking is responsible for about 4,000 deaths ... among people under age 21 each year."* (20) It is estimated that annually in the U.S., *"about 696,000 students ages 18 to 24 are assaulted by another student who has been drinking."* (21)

The manufacturers of the substance are able to donate to political parties and, thereby, encourage a minimally restrictive legislative environment in relation to the drug. Promotion of the drug is omnipresent in the media and it is advertised in association with sport and other pursuits that young people are attracted to. It is routinely placed in television shows to normalise and, thereby, encourage its use.

Secondly, if your child chooses to associate with a drug of choice other than alcohol, tobacco and caffeine, they are criminalised and, therefore, liable to involvement in the criminal justice system. This criminalisation exists solely to provide a resource of people to be exploited in order to enable financial gain and political advantage. If your child is convicted of a crime in relation to possessing or supplying an illicit drug this will have a profoundly negative effect on their lives and they will be exploited in a ruthless manner. Their lives will be made difficult and to some extent chaotic due to factors such as difficulty or inability in obtaining employment, housing or insurance, for example.

As a result of the criminalisation of the supply of drugs other than alcohol, tobacco and caffeine, young people are prevented from having access to a legal and regulated supply of substances. This can have negative consequences for their health and welfare as the quality and dose of the drugs they use is unknown.

The GESICC utilises a resource of people who are criminalised as defined by their associations with drugs other than alcohol, tobacco and caffeine for the purpose of economic exploitation. All of these people are someone's children. Parents generally wish for their children to have the best lives possible and vote throughout their lives in the belief that politicians and the policies they implement and oversee have the best interests of their children at heart.

However, many of these parents do not have an understanding of the true intentions of the so-called 'War on Drugs' and, therefore, do not understand that it is a policy designed to aggressively exploit their children with no regard whatsoever for their welfare should they choose to associate with drugs other than alcohol, tobacco and caffeine. It must be understood by parents that the policy portrayed as protecting their children from drug-related harm is entirely malevolent and exploitative and not related in any way to promoting the well-being of their children in relation to the use of psychoactive substances.

AN OPIOID OVERDOSE CRISIS?

The claim that the use of opioids constitutes a threat to the health and welfare of the American people of such magnitude so as to require a nationwide strategy to prevent and minimise use of the substances is one that has no basis in evidence. Furthermore, the claim is clearly baseless from a number of perspectives supported by an indisputable evidential foundation.

Firstly, the most dangerous drug in the United States is tobacco. As stated by the Centers for Disease Control and Prevention, *"Cigarette smoking is estimated to cause ... More than 480,000 deaths annually"* and *"Tobacco use is the leading preventable cause of death in the United States."* (1) Obviously, if a genuine nationwide strategy was deemed to be required in response to a grave threat to health and welfare due to drug use, the drug that would be addressed is tobacco.

Secondly, and as detailed at the beginning of this book, the full opioid-agonist drug morphine in substantial overdose is proven not to cause injury or death due to compromise or cessation of breathing.

Thirdly and specifically regarding 'overdose', the rapidity of metabolism of opioid drugs, in this case morphine, prevents a situation of markedly high blood-levels of the drug occurring. Decades of evidence has

158

demonstrated the presence of low, non-problematic levels of opioid drugs in cases of deaths in which the drug class has been present.

It is well documented that the circumstance which can be life-threatening is dangerous combinations of central nervous system depressant drugs such as alcohol, benzodiazepines or barbiturates, for example, in which opioids are one component. This can cause profound and disabling sedation that can in turn lead to airway obstruction and asphyxiation.

The drug that commonly contributes to injury and death both in isolation and in combination with other depressant drugs is alcohol. However, statistics used to assist in proclaiming the existence of a crisis relating to the use of opioids have been created in such a way so as to disregard the contribution of alcohol to what are termed 'drug overdose deaths'. Codes from the International Statistical Classification of Diseases and Related Health Problems (ICD-10) have been used to collate the figures. (22)

The class described as "*unintentional*" (accidental poisoning by and exposure to noxious substances) includes the codes X40 through to X44. X45 addresses alcohol. The class "*suicide*" (intentional self-harm) includes the codes X60 through to X64. X65 addresses alcohol. Finally, the class "*undetermined*" (event of undetermined intent) includes the codes Y10 through to Y14. Y15 addresses alcohol. (22) The codes for alcohol involvement have been excluded when formulating the statistics.

A common process leading to death in events erroneously described as 'drug overdose' is compromise of breathing caused by airway obstruction in the context of profound sedation brought about by combinations of depressant drugs. These combinations often involve alcohol so, accordingly, omission of the drug from the statistics prevents them from having any credibility whatsoever regarding these events.

The causal nature of mixed-drug toxicity in relation to incidents involving compromise of breathing is universally ignored and incidents involving multiple drugs including opioids are mischievously portrayed as resulting solely from the effects of opioids.

Misleading terminology such as 'opioid overdose death' is at the forefront of reporting of the events by government agencies and the media in the United States and elsewhere. It is generally only in the contents of reports and research that terms such as 'opioid involved' and 'opioid related' are encountered. These terms convey a reluctant admission that most adverse events represented as being due to overdoses of opioids involve the presence of other substances.

Some countries are more willing to convey the reality of the situation: *"In addition, available data suggest that approximately 80% of accidental apparent opioid-related deaths ... also involved one or more types of non-opioid substances."* (23) An *"apparent opioid-related death"* is described as being *"caused by an intoxication/toxicity (poisoning) resulting from substance use, where one or more of the substances is an opioid"*. (23) Although acknowledging the presence of other drugs, the statements accentuate the presence of opioids in drug combinations at the expense of the salient issue which is the mixing of depressant drugs.

Obviously, the strategy portrayed as a response to what is often called an 'opioid overdose epidemic' has intentions other than those stated. There are a multitude of healthcare-related entities that stand to gain from the further maligning of opioids and the supply of the drugs being restricted. A brief analysis of who can benefit from the strategy can assist in providing an indication as to its true intentions and its role in reinforcing the GESICC.

The strategy provides the basis upon which to further reinforce the falsehood of opioids being a unique threat to health and welfare. The continued maligning of opioids also provides apparent justification for the aggressive and unrelenting measures in regard to supply and possession employed under the GESICC.

The strategy is portrayed as being required to further restrict the supply of opioids including those originating from regulated sources such as medical opioids. Minimising the diversion of medical opioids protects the value and vitality of the black market in non-medical opioids. It also provides work for agencies such as the Drug Enforcement Administration in the United States which is funded by public money and whose work involves reducing the supply of drugs other than alcohol, tobacco and caffeine.

The Drug Enforcement Administration has the ability to set production quotas for opioid medications. The agency *"limits the quantity of Schedule I and II controlled substances ... that may be produced in the United States ... for legitimate medical, scientific and research needs, inventory, and lawful exports."* (6 pp. 14-15) Those wishing to supply or prescribe controlled substances such as opioids must be registered with the DEA. (6 p.11)

The protection of the black market in opioids and, consequently, the provision of work to government agencies such as the DEA has manifested in an extremely aggressive manner with doctors and others being pursued and prosecuted when it is deemed they have supplied opioids in amounts indicative of diversion to recreational users. This has resulted in many medical practitioners being reluctant to prescribe opioid medications resulting in patients being untreated or under-treated for pain. It is routine for patients to be referred to so-called 'pain clinics' as doctors divest themselves of patients receiving opioid therapy due to provision of the drugs being made administratively and legally troublesome.

In relation to the distribution of public money to areas not associated with enforcement in the U.S., the State Opioid Response (SOR) and Tribal Opioid Response (TOR) grant programs *"will award nearly $3 billion over two years to help states and tribes provide community-level resources for people in need of prevention, treatment and recovery support services."* (24) This is in line with the strategy of deeming use of a drug other than alcohol, tobacco and caffeine as a wholly negative and harmful phenomenon thereby providing the grounds upon which to distribute public money in order to create employment and, accordingly, political advantage.

The strategy has provided a rich bounty for the legal profession courtesy of legal action taken against pharmaceutical companies by governments and others. Individuals such as physicians defending themselves after being prosecuted or denied registration by federal agencies and patients attempting to secure treatment can also provide work for legal practitioners. Legal action against pharmaceutical companies has led to substantial monetary settlements being secured from which many seek to benefit.

Those providing apparent alternative treatment modalities for pain have potentially found benefit in the provision of opioids being denied, restricted and discouraged. Pharmaceutical companies manufacturing non-opioid pain medications and non-pharmacological treatment modalities, allied and alternative health providers and others providing apparent alternatives for the treatment of pain stand to benefit from the restriction and maligning of opioid medications.

As an example of commercial advantage being sought in an environment of anti-opioid hysteria, a local anaesthetic is being marketed with great fanfare on the basis that it is 'opioid free'. Bupivacaine is routinely injected into a wound by surgeons to provide post-operative pain relief. A long-acting version of the substance is being promoted for its potential in reducing post-surgical opioid use.

However, bupivacaine is cardiotoxic. It has been associated with adverse cardiac events which can be life threatening. This is a stark indication of the overall safety of opioids. No medication is risk free and opioids are troublesome due to nausea and constipation but they do not carry the risk of serious adverse events such as cardiac complications.

The parties benefiting from what is represented as being an 'opioid overdose crisis' are many and varied but there is one relationship that is relatively significant. Opioid provision forms a highly lucrative market for the pharmaceutical industry. The criminalisation of the supply of recreational opioids affords some degree of commercial advantage. This situation gives them exclusive rights to legally supply the drugs for applications such as opioid substitution therapy and this market dominance is threatened only by opioids supplied by the black market.

In summary, a situation is being alleged in which a significant number of people are dying due to the simple act of taking an excessive amount of an opioid drug. This is not and cannot be the case. There is no evidence that an overdose of opioids can lead to injury or death due to compromise or cessation of breathing. There is only evidence indicating such a scenario is not a reality.

The evidence in relation to injury and death due to compromise of breathing in drug-related incidents in which opioids are involved is that dangerous combinations of central nervous system depressant drugs are implicated. The chain of events involved in this situation is profound and disabling sedation due to a combination of different classes of depressant drugs leading to airway obstruction and asphyxiation.

There is no 'opioid overdose crisis'. It is simply a strategy, in part, to create fear by reinforcing the incorrect portrayal of opioids as a uniquely dangerous class of drugs. This supports the portrayal of governments as protecting the health and welfare of the populace by continuing to prosecute the policy represented as a war on drugs.

The primary element desired by governments is maintenance of the criminalisation of supply and possession of recreational opioids. This facilitates the distribution of public money and, thereby, the attainment of political advantage along with the continuance of the highly lucrative black market in opioids. Those who use opioids on a recreational basis continue to be economically utilised as a criminalised minority.

The strategy adds a dimension whereby a host of commercial healthcare-related entities stand to gain from the restriction of the supply of medical opioids and their use being maligned. Those who use opioids for medical reasons are consequently utilised on an economic basis by being denied or having restricted a medication that treats their symptoms such as pain safely and effectively.

If there was no so-called 'War on Drugs', there would be no phenomenon represented as a crisis in relation to opioid use as there is no proclamation of a crisis relating to tobacco or alcohol use.

MUSIC, DANCE AND HEAT

In the summers of 2017 to 2019, six young people died after attending music festivals in New South Wales (a state of Australia). Officially, the deaths were universally attributed solely or partly to the use of MDMA (ecstasy). In the coroner's report, MDMA toxicity was cited as the single cause of death in four cases with one case described as being due to complications of MDMA use and one as mixed-drug toxicity involving MDMA and cocaine. (25 pp. 132-134) There was no mention in the formal findings of hyperthermia, alcohol or caffeine as contributing factors to the deaths. Alcohol was detected in toxicology results in two cases and alcohol use was reported anecdotally in four cases. (25 p.19) Combined alcohol and caffeine consumption was reported anecdotally in one case. (25 p.40)

A common factor in the deaths was hyperthermia (high body temperature) with one person's temperature recorded as being in excess of 43 °C which is unequivocally life threatening. (25 p.37) The patients were treated onsite, in transit and in hospital for hyperthermia and conditions occurring as a consequence of it. In one case, the presence of hyponatraemia was indicated which is a potentially fatal condition often associated with excessive water consumption.

Environmental conditions at the festivals were typified by high ambient temperatures and some of the venues were outdoors with limited shade. These were music and dance events so, accordingly, there was a situation of strenuous physical activity in the context of high ambient temperatures including direct sunlight at the outdoor events. The occurrence of fatal and non-fatal hyperthermia in this setting is, therefore, unsurprising and completely foreseeable.

There are several points of interest arising from the deaths of the six young people that are worthy of discussion in the context of current policy that is represented as a war on drugs and as having the intention of protecting health and welfare.

Firstly, despite the evidence implicating environmentally-related hyperthermia in the incidents, the deaths were attributed solely to illicit drugs (in particular, MDMA). As regards hyperthermia, there is no evidence that consumption of MDMA is associated with an increase in body temperature other than of a minor and non life-threatening nature. If it was the case that the drug caused dangerous hyperthermia due to a biological process in low or moderate ambient temperatures with an absence of strenuous physical activity there would be a significant body of evidence indicating the existence of such a phenomenon.

Secondly, the primary recommendation in relation to preventing further occurrences of deaths at indoor and outdoor music festivals with the established potential for high ambient temperatures, strenuous physical activity and poly-substance use was pill testing. It would seem reasonable in the circumstances to concentrate first and foremost on the danger of holding these events at the height of the Australian summer: conditions that are obviously conducive to the occurrence of potentially fatal heat-related illness.

If pill testing is commenced on a consistent and entrenched basis, it would become another industry that is reliant upon the criminalisation of the supply of drugs other than alcohol, tobacco and caffeine and, therefore, the oppression of a minority. It would therefore become another industry reliant upon a human-rights abuse for its very existence and its proponents could be expected to be in favour of the continuance of the policies that provide the basis for their industry.

The official recommendation for the introduction of pill testing was greeted with great enthusiasm by those wishing to profit from it including specialist providers and advocacy groups. Little enthusiasm was displayed in regard to initiating discussion about the obvious concern in relation to the deaths being hyperthermia related to environmental factors.

Thirdly, there appeared to be little overt concern regarding the situation that exists in which the young are obliged to obtain one of their drugs of choice from the black market and, therefore, in a form that is unregulated in relation to its manufacture. Obviously, if MDMA was supplied in a legal and regulated manner, services such as pill testing would be irrelevant.

Finally, the fact that the most dangerous drug for the young (alcohol) is supplied to patrons as a matter of course at these events and yet this is worthy only of brief discussion. This is indicative of the duplicitous nature of the laws and policies concerned with the supply and possession of psychoactive substances.

The deaths were surrounded by a maelstrom of public discourse comprised of the usual denial, dishonesty and self-interest. Themes such as the dangers of illicit drugs, pill testing and decriminalisation were at the forefront of a conversation that appeared to studiously avoid any candid discussion regarding conditions such as exertional heat illness.

Predictably, the course of action chosen by government was to, with conviction, continue on with the policy of criminalisation of supply and possession of drugs other than alcohol, tobacco and caffeine. Universal attribution of the deaths solely or partly to MDMA use despite the involvement of environmentally-related hyperthermia in the incidents and the presence of the drugs alcohol and caffeine in some of the incidents could be interpreted as being a disturbing situation.

The entire aftermath of the young people's deaths was typified by a disturbing indifference regarding the situation of environmentally-related hyperthermia being implicated in the incidents. Despite any contribution of heat-related illness to the deaths, the young people's misfortune was attributed solely to associations with illicit drugs. This occurred in the presence of indications that illicit drugs were not the primary causal factor in relation to the incidents.

CANNABIS

In relation to drugs other than alcohol, tobacco and caffeine, cannabis is generally accepted as the most used substance. As a significant number of people use the drug, a strong movement exists to advocate for the removal of laws that criminalise associations with it. The greater the number of people in a movement the stronger it is in relation to monetary resources and, consequently, political influence.

A narrative utilised to help effect change in the legal status of associations with the drug involves it being portrayed as apparently less dangerous than other illicit substances. It is represented as possessing qualities that make it suitable for the treatment of various ailments. The promotion of its alleged suitability as a medication in the U.S. is likely borne out of the desire to have its place in the Controlled Substances Act moved from Schedule 1 to a less restrictive schedule that acknowledges "*a currently accepted medical use in treatment in the United States.*" (6 p.9)

Those wishing for associations with the substance to not be classed as an offence or for existing penalties to be made less severe are being progressively more successful in achieving their goals. In terms of its danger to health and welfare, since the vast majority of cannabis is smoked and often in combination with tobacco, use of the drug in this manner involves the same fundamental risks as does the smoking of tobacco. As driven by the principles of self-interest, its proponents will portray it as being safer and as having more medical utility than other illicit drugs regardless of the lack of evidence or the credibility of the evidence they offer in support of their claims.

But of course, the actual rationale for making associations with the drug subject to criminal sanctions was not at all related to preventing or minimising harm to health and welfare. It was and is about creating a criminal underclass to be exploited for financial gain and political advantage along with the existence and maintenance of a highly profitable black market in the substance.

It is important to note that the increasing liberalisation of laws relating to the supply and possession of cannabis relate to one factor only: the number of and, therefore, the political power of those who use the substance. It is not related to its comparative potential harm to health and welfare or potential for use as a substance with alleged medical utility.

The age-old strategy employed to generate fear in the mind of the voting public in relation to cannabis is the suggestion that the drug has a causal relationship with schizophrenia. There is not and never has been any evidence indicative of such a relationship. The rate of occurrence of the disorder has remained at approximately one percent of the population and there has not been any statistical correlation between the prevalence of cannabis use and rates of the disorder demonstrated despite the substance being in use for centuries.

The strategy employed by those wishing to create fear, especially amongst parents, is to publish research in which the subjects are aged in their teens and that implies cannabis use has a causal relationship with the disorder. The research is largely in the form of meta-analysis which involves interpreting the data from multiple existing and largely uncontrolled studies in a theoretical manner.

Regarding the basis for research relating to cannabis use and an alleged link to schizophrenia, the researchers have had no way of controlling for any genetic component to the disorder. It is therefore not possible to conduct research with any valid control in relation to a genetic predisposition for the disorder as would be required before any suggestion was made as to causal relationships with environmental factors such as drug use. The studies are generally uncontrolled in relation to the use of recreational drugs other than cannabis.

Regardless of there being no body of evidence suggesting cannabis use causes or 'precipitates' schizophrenia and the studies being unable to provide any proof of a causal relationship, the so-called 'research' is released widely on a regular basis. It is eagerly disseminated via the media with the simple association of the themes cannabis, schizophrenia and young people being sufficient to cause fear and concern amongst parents and the broader population.

Of course, the strategy is to portray the substance as a threat to health and welfare, especially concerning the young, with a view to reinforcing the falsehood of supply and possession of drugs other than alcohol, tobacco and caffeine being criminalised as a response to harm caused to health and welfare. The emotive components of young people and mental illness are utilised to heighten alarm amongst parents and, thereby, elicit their support for the policy that is represented as a war on drugs.

In summary, efforts to reduce the severity of the penalties for supply and possession of cannabis and, ultimately, to remove its status as a controlled substance will gather momentum and be increasingly successful. This will be at the expense of the continued criminalisation of associations with drugs whose users have far less political power and influence simply due to their lower numbers.

OPEN LETTER

To the President, those who control the political processes and the people of the United States of America.

I request that you please cease the global economic system and human-rights atrocity based upon intentionally-created crime known as the 'War on Drugs'.

For fifty years now, a minority as defined by their associations with drugs other than alcohol, tobacco and caffeine have been subject to criminalisation for the purpose of enabling financial gain and political advantage. This has resulted in them being subject to sanctions such as arrest, fines, imprisonment, mandated interventions described as treatment and execution. They have been denied a legal and regulated supply of their drug of choice and, otherwise, oppressed in general.

Our political structures, the criminal justice system and society in general has been corrupted and poisoned by the policy, and the hostility and oppression imposed upon the criminalised minority continues to define humanity as being brutal and mercenary.

There is now an urgent requirement for us to work together in an open and honest manner to meet the challenges that confront us. Continuing to prey upon our fellow man in order to achieve financial gain and political advantage is not a humane, constructive or sustainable way of living and it prevents us from attaining a more civilised existence. Two simple circumstances will enable the end of a worldwide human-rights atrocity.

Firstly, no person being criminalised due to an association (whether possession, use or lawful supply) with a psychoactive substance of any kind taken for its effects on the central nervous system in a non-medical context. Accompanying this situation is the existence of a legal and regulated supply of all psychoactive substances without exception. Secondly, the distribution of public money not being based upon the criminalisation and subsequent economic utilisation of any person.

An economic system based upon intentionally-created crime enabled by the criminalisation and subsequent economic utilisation of a minority is not a humane or justifiable situation and we cannot dare call ourselves civilised while it exists.

So that we can all live in a more equitable and peaceful world, and for the sake of humanity, please put an end to the worldwide policy regime referred to as the 'War on Drugs'.

Yours sincerely and in hope,

Matthew Fraser

POST SCRIPT

At the beginning of this book I documented my first memory of the chilling barbarity of the 'War on Drugs' which was the execution of two people involved in the supply of an illicit substance. What does killing some people who choose to be involved in the supply of heroin, for example, achieve? First and foremost, it assists in restricting the supply of the drug which helps maintain the value and vibrancy of the black market in opioids.

Secondly, it reinforces the misrepresentation of the substance as a uniquely dangerous recreational drug due to extreme measures apparently being justified to minimise its supply and use. This in turn fosters public support for the strategy represented as a war on drugs. Executing some people involved in the supply chain satisfies a number of objectives that have the common aim of reinforcing and perpetuating the global economic system based upon intentionally-created crime known as the 'War on Drugs'.

For those concerned about a lack of reference to the synthetic opioid fentanyl, I have described at length the evidence that exists demonstrating that substantial overdose of heroin and, therefore, its primary active metabolite and full opioid-agonist drug morphine does not result in harm. Fentanyl is a full opioid-agonist drug and the same requirement for safe use applies to it as applies to other opioid drugs: the avoidance of dangerous combinations of central nervous system depressant drugs.

I would like to take this opportunity to reiterate for a final time the fundamental message conveyed in this book. The policy regime popularly referred to as the 'War on Drugs' is not concerned in any way with preventing and minimising harm due to the use of psychoactive substances. To be considered as a response to the harmful effects of drug use, it would have to address the supply and use of alcohol, tobacco and caffeine in the same manner it addresses the supply and use of other drugs.

The so-called 'War on Drugs' is simply a global economic system based upon intentionally-created crime. The crime consists solely of an association with drugs other than alcohol, tobacco and caffeine. The policy facilitates political advantage and financial gain by way of the false portrayal of drugs other than alcohol, tobacco and caffeine as being a unique threat to health and welfare, the allocation of vast amounts of public money and the money generated by the worldwide black market in substances presently deemed to be illicit.

The policy regime represented as a war on drugs is not concerned in any way with addressing drug-related harm: it is solely an economic construct that facilitates financial gain and political advantage through the criminalisation and subsequent economic utilisation of a minority.

179

REFERENCES

The references are ordered as they appear in the text.

1.   Centres for Disease Control and Prevention (Last reviewed Apr. 2020) *Tobacco-related mortality*. [Online] Available at: https://archive.cdc.gov/www_cdc_gov/tobacco /data_statistics/fact_sheets/health_effects/tobacco_related_ mortality/index.htm

2.   A.W. Miser, L. Moore, R. Greene, R.H. Gracely and J.S. Miser. (1986) *Prospective study of continuous intravenous and subcutaneous morphine infusions for therapy-related or cancer-related pain in children and young adults with cancer*. PDF document. The Clinical Journal of Pain, Vol. 2, No. 2 (pp. 101-106) © Raven Press, New York. Available at: https://journals.lww.com/clinicalpain/abstract/1986/02020/ prospective_ study_of_ continuous_intravenous_and.5.aspx

3.   Rook, Elisabeth J. et al. (2006) *Pharmacokinetics and pharmacodynamics of high doses of pharmaceutically prepared heroin, by intravenous or by inhalation route in opioid-dependent patients*. PDF document. © Basic and Clinical Pharmacology and Toxicology 98 (pp. 86-96). Available at: https://onlinelibrary.wiley.com/doi/10.1111 /j.1742-7843.2006.pto_233.x

4.   Zador D, Sunjic S and Darke S. (1996) *Heroin-related deaths in New South Wales, 1992: toxicological findings and circumstances*. © The Medical Journal of Australia, Volume 164, Issue 4 (pp. 204-207). [Online] Available at: https://www.mja.com.au/journal/1996/164/4/heroin-related-deaths-new-south-wales-1992-toxicological-findings-and

5.   *President Nixon Declares Drug Abuse "Public Enemy Number One"*. (2016) [Video] USA: Richard Nixon Foundation. [Online] Available at: https://www.youtube.com/watch?v=y8TGLLQlD9M

6.   Drug Enforcement Administration (2020) *Drugs of abuse*. PDF document. Available at: https://www.dea.gov/sites/default/files/2020-04/Drugs%20of%20Abuse%202020-Web%20Version-508%20compliant-4-24-20_0.pdf

7.   World Health Assembly, 6. (1953) *Medical use of diacetylmorphine (heroin): submitted by the Delegation of the United States of America*. PDF document. World Health Organization. Available at: https://apps.who.int/iris/handle/10665/101785

8.   *Joint Resolution proposing an amendment to the Constitution of the United States*. [N.D.] [Image] [Online] Available at: https://www.wikidata.org/wiki/Q156784

9.   United Nations Office on Drugs and Crime *Policy on Drugs*. [Online] Available at: https://www.unodc.org/unodc/en/commissions/CND/Mandate_Functions/policy-on-drugs.html (Accessed Apr. 2024)

10.   *What is scheduling?* (2019) [Video] United Nations Office on Drugs and Crime. [Online] Available at: https://www.youtube.com/watch/?v=0z_42vNmDEU

11.   Kilmer B, Everingham S, Caulkins J, Midgette G, Pacula R, Reuter P, Burns R, Han B and Lundberg R. (2014) *How Big Is the U.S. Market for Illegal Drugs?* PDF document. Santa Monica, CA: RAND Corporation. Available at: https://www.rand.org/pubs/research_briefs/RB9770.html.

12.   The White House, Executive Office of the President, Office of National Drug Control Policy (2024) *National drug control budget FY 2025 funding highlights*. PDF document. Available at: https://www.whitehouse.gov/wp-content/uploads/2024/03/FY-2025-Budget-Highlights.pdf

13.   Drug Enforcement Administration (2015) *DEA fact sheet*. PDF document. Available at: https://www.dea.gov/sites/default/files/docs/factsheet.pdf

14.   Drug Enforcement Administration *DEA domestic arrests*. [Online] Available at: https://www.dea.gov/data-and-statistics/domestic-arrests (Accessed Apr. 2024)

15.   Drug Enforcement Administration *Staffing and budget*. [Online] Available at: https://www.dea.gov/data-and-statistics/staffing-and-budget (Accessed Apr. 2024)

16.   Carson, EA and Kluckow, R. (2023) *Prisoners in 2022 - statistical tables*. PDF document. Bureau of Justice Statistics, Office of Justice Programs, U.S. Department of Justice. Available at: https://bjs.ojp.gov/

17.   Motivans M, McGilton M, Adams W, Samuels J and Kelly J. (2023) *Sentencing decisions for persons in federal prison for drug offenses, 2013-2018*. PDF document. Bureau of Justice Statistics, Office of Justice Programs, U.S. Department of Justice. Available at: https://bjs.ojp.gov/

18.   Public.Law *"Offense" described*. [Online] Available at: https://www.oregonlaws.org/ors/161.505 (Accessed Apr. 2024)

19.   *Drug addiction treatment and recovery act*. (2019) PDF document. Available at: https://sos.oregon.gov/admin /Documents/irr/2020/044text.pdf

20.   Centers for Disease Control and Prevention (Last reviewed Apr. 2024) *Underage drinking*. [Online] Available at: https://www.cdc.gov/alcohol/fact-sheets/underage-drinking .htm

21.   National Institute on Alcoholism and Alcohol Abuse (Updated Jan. 2024) *Harmful and underage college drinking*. [Online] Available at: https://www.niaaa.nih.gov /publications/brochures-and-fact-sheets/college-drinking

22.   Ahmak FB, Cisewski JA, Rossen LM and Sutton P. (Last reviewed Apr. 2024) *Provisional Drug Overdose Death Counts*. National Center for Health Statistics, Centers for Disease Control and Prevention. [Online] Available at: https://www.cdc.gov/nchs/nvss/vsrr/drug-overdose-data.htm

23.   Special Advisory Committee on the Epidemic of Opioid Overdoses (2013) *National report: Apparent opioid-related deaths in Canada (January 2016 to September 2017)*. Ottawa: Public Health Agency of Canada. [Online] Available at: https://www.canada.ca/en/public-health/services /publications/healthy-living/national-report-apparent-opioid-related-deaths-released-march-2018.html

24.   U.S Department of Health and Human Services (2020) *HHS releases $1.5 billion to states, tribes to combat opioid crisis.* [Online] Available at: https://www.samhsa.gov /newsroom/press-announcements/202008270530

25.   State Coroner's Court of New South Wales (2019) *Inquest into the death of six patrons of NSW music festivals.* PDF document. Available at: https://coroners.nsw.gov.au /documents/findings/2019/Music_Festival_Redacted_findings _in_the_joint_inquest_into_deaths_arising_at_music_festivals _.pdf

Addendum. The author is aware that the U.S. state of Oregon has decided to reintroduce criminal penalties for possession of small amounts of controlled substances by way of the introduction of a misdemeanour crime of unlawful possession of a controlled substance. The new penalty becomes effective Sept. 1st 2024. The section addressing Measure 110 in Oregon remains entirely relevant in relation to the nature of decriminalisation measures.